Sacred Perthshire and the Tay Valley

SACRED PLACES SERIES

Sacred Perthshire and the Tay Valley

SCOTLAND'S CHURCHES SCHEME

SAINT ANDREW PRESS
Edinburgh

First published in 2011 by
SAINT ANDREW PRESS
121 George Street
Edinburgh EH2 4YN

The cover photograph is of St Adamnan's, Kilmaveonaig, Blair Atholl

A. Stewart Brown: 9, 61, 66, 70, 117, 119, 128; David Gauld: 94; Raymond Parks: 86, 109, 113; Simpson & Brown: 47. All other images by SCS member churches.

ISBN 978 0 7152 0956 1

British Library Cataloguing in Publication Data
A catalogue record for this book is available from the British Library.

It is the publisher's policy to only use papers that are natural and recyclable and that have been manufactured from timber grown in renewable, properly managed forests. All of the manufacturing processes of the papers are expected to conform to the environmental regulations of the country of origin.

Typeset in Enigma by Waverley Typesetters, Warham, Norfolk
Manufactured in Great Britain by Bell & Bain Ltd, Glasgow

BUCKINGHAM PALACE

As Patron of Scotland's Churches Scheme, I warmly welcome this publication as part of the *Sacred Places* series of books being produced by the Scheme.

The story of the heritage and culture of Scotland would be lacking significantly without a strong focus on its churches and sacred sites. I am sure that this guidebook will be a source of information and enjoyment both to the people of Scotland and to our visitors.

Anne

Scotland's Churches Scheme

www.sacredscotland.org.uk

Scotland's Churches Scheme is an ecumenical charitable trust, providing an opportunity to access the nation's living heritage of faith by assisting the 'living' churches in membership to:

- Promote spiritual understanding by enabling the public to appreciate all buildings designed for worship and active as living churches
- Work together with others to make the Church the focus of the community
- Open their doors with a welcoming presence
- Tell the story of the building (however old or new), its purpose and heritage (artistic, architectural and historical)
- Provide information for visitors, young and old

The Scheme has grown rapidly since its inception in 1994, and there are now more than 1,200 churches in membership. These churches are to be found across all parts of Scotland and within all the denominations.

The *Sacred Scotland* theme promoted by Scotland's Churches Scheme focuses on the wish of both visitors and local communities to be able to access our wonderful range of church buildings in a meaningful way, whether the visit be occasioned by spiritual or heritage motivation or both. The Scheme can advise and assist member churches on visitor welcome, and, with its range of 'how-to' brochures, provide information on research, presentation, security and other live issues relating to the buildings and associated graveyards. With its network of local representatives, the Scheme encourages the opening of doors and the care of tourists and locals alike, and offers specific services such as the provision of grants for organ-playing.

Sacred Scotland (www.sacredscotland.org.uk), the website of Scotland's Churches Scheme, opens the door to Scotland's story by exploring living traditions of faith in city, town, village and island across the country. The site is a portal to access information on Scotland's churches of all denominations and is a starting point for your special journeys.

The Scheme has also embarked, with support from Scottish Enterprise and Historic Scotland, on the identification and promotion of Scotland's Pilgrim Ways, with the huge resource of its expanding website and database of sacred sites. With the growing awareness and enthusiasm for such an initiative, a pilot project is already under way and is seen as a welcome development of the Scheme's existing activity and publications.

We are delighted to be working with Saint Andrew Press in the publication of this *Sacred Places* series of regional guides to Scotland's churches. In 2009, the first three volumes were published – *Sacred South-West Scotland; Sacred Edinburgh and Midlothian;* and *Sacred Fife and the Forth Valley*. In 2010, a further three volumes were published – *Sacred Borders and East Lothian; Sacred Glasgow and the Clyde Valley*; and *Sacred North-East Scotland*. This volume, *Sacred Perthshire and the Tay Valley*, is one of the final three to be published in 2011, now covering the whole country. The others are *Sacred Argyll and Clyde* and *Sacred Highlands and Islands*. We are grateful to the authors of the introductory articles, Professor John Hume, one of our trustees, and Kenneth Steven, for their expert contributions to our understanding of sacred places.

The growth of 'spiritual tourism' worldwide is reflected in the million-plus people who visit Scotland's religious sites annually. We hope that the information in this book will be useful in bringing alive the heritage as well as the ministry of welcome which our churches offer. In the words of our former President, Lady Marion Fraser: 'we all owe a deep debt of gratitude to the many people of vision who work hard and imaginatively to create a lasting and peaceful atmosphere which you will carry away with you as a special memory when you leave'.

Dr Brian Fraser
Director, Scotland's Churches Scheme
Dunedin, Holehouse Road, Eaglesham, Glasgow G76 0JF

Scotland's Churches Scheme: local representatives

Dr Andrew Dawson (*Angus and Dundee*)
Mrs Nancy Johnston (*Perthshire*)

Invitation to Pilgrimage

Perthshire and the Tay Valley

I don't deny that I have a tendency to think of pilgrimage in the context of the west coast of Scotland. Since my earliest childhood, Iona has been the end of the journey – and, because Iona is difficult to access, being two islands removed from the mainland, it has reinforced that sense of pilgrimage. For ten years, I was the co-leader of a writing course on the island, and each time we regathered we considered the journey that had brought us there. At the heart of the week's meditations was the nature of pilgrimage, and over the years I've found myself asking what pilgrimage means to me, and learning a great deal about what it means to others.

But I live inland, at the heart of Scotland, in Highland Perthshire. It was to here, to Dunkeld Cathedral, that the early remains of St Columba were brought for safe-keeping from the Viking raids on Iona. There's no sense of the sea here; this is an inland world composed of deep glens and wooded hills, wide rivers and winding lochs. Yet, in two important ways, the notion of pilgrimage has come alive for me in this landscape.

The first is through crannogs, those ancient artificial islands on lochs. They were made as places of sanctuary in earliest times, when the surrounding land was impenetrable forest and fierce with wild creatures. An underwater causeway led the returning island-dweller back to the safety of the crannog.

We know just how important islands were to the Celts, how they saw them as holy places. We tend to think of those islands in the context of the coasts: Iona, Lindisfarne and so on. But there's no doubt that inland, freshwater islands could be seen by the Celts as equally special and set apart. Whether they believed the old crannogs to be of spiritual significance, or whether they redefined their purpose, is another matter; the fact is that many became used for chapels and as retreat places – places of pilgrimage.

An island is somewhere set apart. It doesn't have the distractions and the temptations of the mainland; on a small island it becomes easier to listen to one's heart, to focus on the things of the spirit. One is forced into a deeper awareness of existence, of each moment, in elemental terms: the going for water, the finding of wood, the making of the fire. Living is stripped down to the bone, and one's inner and outer existence are brought into far closer harmony.

The people of Dunkeld still talk about a secret path that led from the Cathedral to the island on Loch Clunie where the Bishop's palace stood. (At one time, that island itself had been a crannog; it became the spiritual retreat of the bishops in pre-Reformation times.) The path may not in actual fact have been secret, but it would certainly have been sacred – a pilgrimage route chosen for silent retreat when the pressures of life in the 'little city' of Dunkeld became too much.

I have a greater and greater sense of the journey of the pilgrimage. There is a danger of seeing the pilgrimage as a means to an end, as being all about the destination. The Norwegian author whose work I have translated writes that 'the journey is also a place' – and I have found those words profound and wise. As human beings, we rush to get to new 'somewheres', special destinations; in our rushing, we are almost unaware of the journey. But the journey is our preparation for the destination; it is our re-meeting with God, of whom we may well have begun to lose sight and to forget. It is on the journey that we must practise the leaving behind of the sparkling things of life that distract and deflect us. It is a struggle; like children, we must put down the things we have put down in the past (perhaps many times before). Each day is a beginning afresh. In this way, we have a chance of reaching the island, the crannog, ready to live within its simplicity.

There is another sense of pilgrimage that has come to fascinate me here at the heart of Scotland, and that is the pilgrimage to wells. I think that some of these ceremonial processions must be truly ancient, perhaps going back right to the Bronze Age. There is a well above the Blairgowrie moors called the Santa Crux; it sits in a landscape littered with ancient sites – early dwellings, field systems and standing stones. At one time, on the first Sunday of May, there would be a procession of thousands to the well; people came from as far away as France to drink the water and to take part in the service held for the sick. For what could be more wonderful than a tongue of pure water spouting from the ground itself, from the heart of the earth?

The Celts took these superstitious marches at the ushering in of summer in the old pagan calendar, and they christened them. They linked them to the lives of saints, and to all the significance of wells and water in the New Testament. It's more than likely that the minerals of pure spring water did plenty of good to those who partook of them, in days when life truly could be nasty, brutish and short.

It's my earnest hope that such pilgrimages can be rediscovered in our time. Not because we need the water; in our rich western world, we can have a cornucopia of supplements and minerals brought to our door. No, it's because I think we need the pilgrimage.

In little Scotland, where division between and within denominations and between churches and unchurched can seem insuperable, we desperately need pilgrimages where we can learn to walk together, literally and metaphorically speaking. We are united in our following of Christ and of his path, but how often would you know it? In re-establishing and re-enacting pilgrimage, we have the chance to lay to one side the things that niggle and to focus on the path and on the journey that unites. The journey is also a place, and here it has the chance to be a place of learning and sharing and growing.

The Well

I found a well once
In the dark green heart of a wood.

I stretched down, cupped a deep handful
Out of the winter darkness of its world

And drank. That water tasted of moss, of secrets,
Of ancient meetings, of laughter,

Of dark stone, of crystal –
It reached the roots of my being,

Assuaged a whole summer of thirst.
I have been wandering for that water ever since.

(From the collections *Iona* and *Island: Selected Poems*, both Saint Andrew Press)

Kenneth Steven
Dunkeld

Introduction

Sacred Perthshire and the Tay Valley

This area can truthfully be described as the heart of Scotland. It is traversed by the River Tay, which runs, fully formed, out of Loch Tay. On its way to the North Sea, the Tay is joined by numerous tributary streams, notably the Tummel and the Earn. At Dundee, the river widens into an estuary and then into the Firth of Tay. Fife forms the south bank of the estuary and firth, and on the north bank is the county of Angus, with the city of Dundee on its western margin. The northern edges of Perthshire and Angus are Highland in character, with narrow glens along the north-western side of the Highland boundary fault. To the south and east are fertile, well-drained areas with relatively low rainfall. These were settled early in Scotland's prehistory, and the lowland areas of Perth, Kinross and Angus are still attractive places in which to live. There is only one city, Dundee, in the area covered in this volume, but a number of old towns – Perth, Arbroath, Montrose, Forfar, Blairgowrie and Rattray – and two new ones created by nineteenth-century tourism, Crieff and Pitlochry. There are also several smaller urban settlements, such as Dunkeld, Aberfeldy, Kirriemuir, Alyth and Errol, and many villages and hamlets. The whole area is largely agricultural: arable in the lowland parts and pastoral in the Highlands, with sporting estates complementing the latter.

All the larger settlements grew in the eighteenth and nineteenth centuries partly or largely as centres of textile manufacture – linen and jute in the east, and woollen in the west. The bleaching of cotton and linen cloth was a notable

Fig. 1. Round tower, Abernethy, Perth & Kinross

Fig. 2. The former Muthill Parish Church, Perth & Kinross

industry in the vicinity of Perth. Apart from the city of Dundee, the area was little affected by migration from Ireland, but the opportunities offered by the textile industries led to internal migration from the eastern Highlands and from more rural parts of the area. Dundee has shared with other Scottish cities the decline of traditional industries and the need to rehouse people from overcrowded Victorian inner areas. Thus Dundee's centre is ringed by housing estates built on greenfield sites from the 1920s to the 1960s, though some of these are now being redeveloped for a second time. There is no coal in the area, so that it was reliant on coastwise shipment of coal until railways were built to serve it from the late 1840s. This very summary account of the physical and human geography of the area is necessary background to an understanding of its church history.

The spiritual importance of the area can be dated back to the Bronze Age, when a ritual enclosure on a immense scale was constructed from timber in the vicinity of Forteviot, in Strathearn. This seems to have had considerable prestige in later pre-Christian times, overlapping with the earliest physical evidence of Christianity in the area, which is the body of Pictish stones found all over the lowland parts of Perthshire and Angus. Some of these stones are among the finest Dark Ages sculpture in western Europe. Examples include the Dunfallandy, Aberlemno Churchyard, Glamis Manse and Eassie stones, while the Dupplin Cross, now in St Serf's Church, Dunning, is an unusual instance of a cross-shaped Pictish stone. In Meigle and at St Vigeans, there are outstanding collections of early Christian sculptured stones. Many of the larger Pictish stones seem

Fig. 3. The former St Serf's Parish Church, Dunning, Perth & Kinross

Fig. 4. Arbroath Abbey, Angus

to be symbols of the occupation of land by settled agricultural communities. There are no complete first-generation stone churches in the area, but elements of twelfth-century or earlier churches survive as parts of more recent buildings, or in association with them. Notable early features include the two round towers at Brechin (eleventh century, **9**) and Abernethy (later eleventh century, Fig. 1), indications of Irish-Celtic influence. The square towers at Muthill (twelfth century, Fig. 2) and St Serf's, Dunning (c. 1200, Fig. 3) are comparable with the Fife towers of St Rule's, St Andrews, and Markinch Parish Church. The remains of Restenneth Priory incorporate pre-Romanesque masonry. The body of St Serf's, Dunning also incorporates early masonry. Parts of St Vigeans Church (twelfth–thirteenth century and later, **4**) are Romanesque, and there is a Romanesque archway of about 1200 in the kirkyard of Collace (**78**).

From the Gothic period, there are the substantial remains of the abbey church of Arbroath (Fig. 4); the cathedral churches of Brechin (thirteenth–fourteenth century, **9**) and Dunkeld (c. 1350, and fifteenth century, **86**, Fig. 5); the great burgh churches of St John's, Perth (1242 on, **108**) and St Mary's, Dundee (steeple, fifteenth century, **58**); the collegiate church of Tullibardine (in the care of Historic Scotland); and the parish churches of St Marnock's, Fowlis Easter (1453 and later, **16**) and Fowlis Wester (thirteenth century and later, **90**), Forgandenny (Fig. 6) and St Mary's, Grandtully, in the care of Historic Scotland. There are other, less well-defined, medieval remains in, among others, the ruined churches of Aberuthven, Inchaffray Abbey (c. 1200 on), Innerpeffray (collegiate church, c. 1507), Ecclesiamagirdle (probably c. 1500) and in the complete but disused church of Tibbermore (1632 on, **127**), now in the care of the Scottish Redundant Churches

Fig. 5. Dunkeld Cathedral, the ruined nave and tower, Perth & Kinross

Fig. 6. Forgandenny Parish Church, Perth & Kinross

Trust. A fine, if neglected, relic of the immediate post-Reformation period is the Gray Aisle, Kinfauns (1598), created by a local landowning family after the Reformers prohibited burials in churches. From the seventeenth century, there are the parish churches of Weem (now a mausoleum, 1609–14 on) and Auchterhouse (1630, **7**), and the massive tower of Longforgan (1690, **102**). At Murthly Castle is a private chapel of about 1600, now a mausoleum. The painted ceilings of St Mary's, Grandtully and of the private chapel of Stobhall also date from the seventeenth century. In Scone Old (**121**) is the magnificent Stormont Pew of 1616. This is a rich heritage, and one that can be seen as spanning the whole of the area covered by this volume. From the early eighteenth century on, however, there are many more surviving churches – and, for convenience of reference, the rest of this Introduction is in sections covering the churches of Angus; the City of Dundee; and Perth and Kinross.

Angus

As mentioned above, the Priory church of Restenneth seems, according to recent research, to incorporate at the base of its tower late first-millennium masonry, probably the oldest Christian fabric in our area. Not much later is the Irish-style tower of Brechin Cathedral, the only intact structure of its type in Scotland (eleventh century, **9**). The collection of Pictish sculptured stones at St Vigeans, near Arbroath, is in a cottage below the mound on which the parish church (**4**) sits. This building incorporates twelfth- and thirteenth-century masonry, but has been much rebuilt. Arbroath Abbey, the area's most celebrated ecclesiastical site, was founded in 1178 by William the Lion, but the remains of the church are later. The other large medieval church in Angus is Brechin Cathedral (thirteenth–fourteenth century, **9**). After the Reformation, the nave

Fig. 7. The former Eassie Parish Church, Angus

Fig. 8. Steeple, Forfar Old Parish Church, Angus

became the parish church, and the choir was not restored until the late nineteenth century. At St Marnock's, Fowlis Easter (1453, **16**), there are important remains of pre-Reformation church furnishings and decoration. At Guthrie (**20**), there is a fifteenth-century detached aisle, and at Glamis the Strathmore Aisle (1459), retained when the church (dedicated to St Fergus) was rebuilt in 1792 (**17**), is used as part of the church premises. The parish church of Lundie, north of Dundee (**31**), restored in 1892, contains medieval masonry; and the ruined church of Eassie (containing a fine Pictish stone) dates in part from the sixteenth century, though it was remodelled in 1753 (Fig. 7). Whether Eassie is pre- or post-Reformation is not clear; but Auchterhouse Parish Church dates from 1630 (**7**) and appears to be largely of that period. Aberlemno, east of Forfar (1722, **1**), has one of the finest Pictish sculptured stones in its graveyard, but the church itself has been much altered since the early eighteenth century.

All of these churches, and the fine sculptured stones, suggest that, at least from the early medieval period, lowland Angus was a prosperous agricultural area. From the 1720s, however, the manufacture of linen cloth seems to have become general throughout the area, and thus resulted in the growth of the towns and villages, and hence of a need for more and larger churches. Agricultural improvement, too, increased the wealth of Angus. The country church of Inverarity (1754, **21**) has become an exemplar for the eighteenth-century Scottish rural church – and very fine it is, too, but not really typical. Airlie (1783, **2**), an estate church, is fairly similar. By the 1780s, however, the towns and villages were beginning to draw population from the

Fig. 9. The former Maryton Parish Church, Montrose, Angus

Fig. 10. Farnell Parish Church, Angus

countryside. In 1772, the first Methodist church in Scotland was built in Arbroath (**6**) – evidence, probably, of English migration into the town. This church is octagonal, in the fashion of the time. It has been much altered. The first large burgh church in Angus was Kirriemuir Old Parish Church (1788–90, **24**), and it was soon followed by Forfar Old (1791) and Montrose Old (1793, **35**). Kirriemuir had a simple Georgian steeple from the first, but the other two churches did not have theirs until later. Forfar's spire (1814, Fig. 8) is based on that of St Andrew's, Dundee, while that of Montrose (1832–4, **35**) is a striking late English Gothic structure, probably designed in part as a navigational aid.

Angus seems to have been in the forefront of the introduction of the early Gothic Revival into Scotland. Maryton (1791, Fig. 9), now a house, and Stracathro (1799, **42**) both have pointed windows, as do St Fergus's, Glamis (1792, **17**) and the little country churches of Glen Prosen (1801–2, **19**) and Lintrathen (1802, **29**). Craig, south of Montrose, is said to have been the first true Gothic Revival church in Scotland (1799). It too is now a house. Farnell (1806, Fig. 10), with its curved castellated frontage, is unique, but foreshadows later versions of the early Gothic ('Gothick') Revival. Most of the new churches built in following years had, however, simple pointed windows, such as Monifieth (1813), Rescobie (1820, **40**), Glenisla (1821, **18**), Guthrie (1826, **20**) and Lethnot and Navar, Edzell (1827, Fig. 11). The last-named is unusual in having a tower with a cast-iron bell frame. Cortachy (1828, **11**), an estate church, breaks this mould, being a jewel-like miniature building in English Perpendicular style. In marked contrast are the area's two classical churches: Arbroath Inverbrothock (1828), very plain and sober (now a gospel church), and St John's Church of Scotland, Montrose (1829), with a fine portico, comparable with the best in Scotland at the time. Within two years, Arbroath Old had been built in an advanced Gothic Revival style. Only its steeple survives, but

Fig. 11. Lethnot and Navar Parish Church, Edzell, Angus

Fig. 12. Knox United Free Church (ex-United Presbyterian), Montrose, Angus

this must have been one of the most innovative churches of its period in Scotland. Though less striking, Liff (1839, **28**) was also in the forefront of the introduction of the steepled Gothic Revival into Scotland, a development of far-reaching implications. Kingoldrum (1840, **23**) seems to have been the last Angus parish church built before the Disruption in 1843.

Though the new Free Church thereby created was warmly embraced in Dundee, it did not have a marked effect on most of Angus. Free churches were speedily built at Memus (Tannadice Free, 1843, **32**) and Muirhead (1843, **38**), and probably in the towns, where they were later replaced by larger churches when finance allowed. Other surviving churches from the 1840s are the striking Roman Catholic church of St Thomas of Canterbury, Arbroath (an unusual dedication) of 1848 (**5**), in a castellated Gothic, and the more conventional Murroes and Tealing (1848, **39**) with Gothic detailing. St Mary's Scottish Episcopal Church, Arbroath (1852–4) is a good 'correct' steepled Gothic building. A notable urban Free church was the West Free, Brechin (1856), with a massive steeple. It was later a Baptist church. Other Gothic country churches are Ruthven (1859, **41**) and Tannadice (1866, **43**), both with little spires. Ruthven also has ornamental slating. Kilry (1876–7, **22**) is a very simple Gothic church.

In the towns, churches named after John Knox, pioneering Reformer, had a vogue perhaps in the aftermath of the 300th anniversary of the Reformation, celebrated in 1860. The former Mill Street United Presbyterian Church, Montrose, now Knox United Free Church (1864, Fig. 12, **37**) and Knox's Free, Arbroath (now Church of Scotland, 1867), are both in a simple Gothic Revival style,

Fig. 13. St Margaret's Parish Church (ex-Forfar Free), Forfar, Angus

Fig. 14. Gardner Memorial Parish Church, Brechin, Angus

virtually standard by that time, as were Monifieth Free (1871) and St Ninian's, Brechin (Roman Catholic, 1875, **10**). The latter, and St John the Evangelist Scottish Episcopal Church, Forfar (1879–81, **14**), are more correctly Gothic than some of their contemporaries. Nevertheless, some of the late Gothic Revival buildings, though not 'correct', are impressive pieces of townscape, such as Forfar Free (now St Margaret's, 1880–1, Fig. 13), St Andrew's Church of Scotland, Arbroath (1885, **3**) and St Andrew's Scottish Episcopal Church, Brechin (1888). By that time, Arbroath, Forfar and Brechin had become significant textile towns. More modest Gothic buildings of this period include St Margaret's Roman Catholic Church, Montrose (1886, **36**) and the Scottish Episcopal Church of the Holy Rood, Carnoustie (1880–1), with its little spire.

As the end of the nineteenth century approached, church design became significantly more original. The Gardner Memorial Church of Scotland, Brechin (1896–1900, Fig. 14) is a superb example, perhaps the best of the 'low-line' churches designed by Glasgow architect Sir J. J. Burnet. In the twentieth century, the outstanding church in the area is the Lowson Memorial Parish Church of Scotland, Forfar (1914, **13**), late Scots Gothic, with a remarkable suite of stained-glass windows. Other fine churches of the period are St Mary's Scottish Episcopal Church, Kirriemuir (1903, **25**) in English 'Arts and Crafts' style, and Holy Trinity Scottish Episcopal Church, Monifieth (1909, **33**), the best of Scotland's half-timbered Arts and Crafts churches. The former United Free Church in Edzell (1900), now demolished, was a good Scots Gothic Arts and Crafts building. Also original, though not so refined, is St Andrew's United Free Church, Kirriemuir (now Church of Scotland, 1903, **26**), like Edzell constructed after the union

Fig. 15. Ward Road Congregational Church (now United Reformed), City of Dundee

Fig. 16. St Mary's Roman Catholic Church, Forebank Road, City of Dundee

between the Free and United Presbyterian churches in 1900. A modest Episcopal church of this period is St Margaret's, Lunanhead (1907, **30**).

Very few churches have been built in Angus since the First World War. When the United Free Church and the Church of Scotland amalgamated in 1929, some members of the former remained independent, and the little Ferryden United Free Church (1935, **12**) was built to serve the fisher families of that village. In 1963, a new Roman Catholic church, St Fergus's, was built in Forfar (**15**), replacing a building of 1846; and two more Roman Catholic churches were constructed in the 1980s, again to replace other buildings. St Bride's, Monifieth (1983, **34**) is a laminated timber-framed building of a near-standard type, but St Anthony's, Kirriemuir (1987, **27**) is a much more original design, still using laminated timber beams.

The City of Dundee

Dundee was an important place in medieval and early modern Scotland as the major port for Perthshire, Angus and north Fife. Buildings which survived into the late nineteenth century testified to the city's wealth in the seventeenth and early eighteenth centuries. The oldest building still extant, the fifteenth-century Steeple (**58**), is the largest of its kind in Scotland. Had it been completed, with its intended crown steeple, it would have been even more impressive. The church of St Mary, of which it was a part, was divided after the Reformation

Fig. 17. The former Victoria Street United Presbyterian Church, City of Dundee

Fig. 18. The Gilfillan Memorial Church, City of Dundee

and subsequently rebuilt in three parts. The older survivor is the Steeple Church (1788, **58**), a simple Gothic building; the newer St Mary's, on the site of the choir of the medieval building, was rebuilt in 1844 (**46**) in full-blooded Gothic Revival.

The significance of Dundee as a port continues, but to that was added, from the later eighteenth century, a linen-manufacturing industry which had become the largest in Britain by the 1830s, and continued to grow. The jute industry grew out of that business and became even larger than the linen trade. Mills were constructed all over the town and in its suburbs, with workers (many of them women) housed in tenements. Irish immigrants formed a significant part of the workforce, and many of them were Roman Catholic. To escape from the dirt and air pollution associated with the jute and linen trades, a large proportion of the city's middle classes chose to live in Broughty Ferry, bracingly sited on the shore of the Firth of Tay. Large numbers of churches were built to serve both Dundee and Broughty Ferry, but many have gone or been adapted for other purposes. All three nineteenth-century Presbyterian denominations – Church of Scotland, Free and United Presbyterian – were well represented, as was the Roman Catholic Church. The Scottish Episcopal Church was unusually strong in the area, and there were also large Congregational, Baptist, Methodist and Independent churches. Much of the city's housing had become insanitary by the early twentieth century, and in the 1920s clearance of older areas, and construction of new local-authority estates on the northern fringe, began, as mentioned above. This process gained momentum after the Second World War. All the new estates had churches provided, sometimes taking their initial congregations from redundant city-centre churches. Demolition of some of the postwar suburbs is

Fig. 19. Menzieshill Parish Church, City of Dundee

being followed by a second wave of new housing, much of it now privately owned.

The consequence of this socio-economic background is that, generally speaking, most of the churches in the area were built either between the 1830s and 1914, or after 1950. The largest eighteenth-century church in Dundee is St Andrew's (1774, **51**), built by the town's merchants and tradesmen, on a commanding site that originally overlooked the harbour. Its tall Georgian steeple was probably intended as a navigational mark. The other is the former Glasite Chapel of 1777, next to St Andrew's, and now serving as that church's halls. Three churches from the 1830s are Ward Congregational Church (1833, Fig. 15), St Andrew's Roman Catholic Cathedral (1835, **48**) and St Peter's Free Church (1836, **56**), built for the Church of Scotland, in a rather out-of-date plain classical style, but becoming a Free church at the Disruption in 1843. The second Roman Catholic church in Dundee was St Mary's, Forebank Road (1850), apparently an externally unremarkable building until a dramatic twin-towered front was added to it in 1900 (Fig. 16). Probably the finest Victorian Roman Catholic church in Scotland is St Mary's, Lochee (1866, **54**), built to serve the people working in the enormous Camperdown Jute Works, then the largest in the world. For the Scottish Episcopal Church, St Paul's Cathedral, enormously tall for its restricted site, was built in 1853 (**47**). Three other churches followed: St Salvador's (1868, **57**), St John the Baptist (1886, **52**) and St Margaret's, Lochee (1888, **53**). St Salvador's has an interior which can be described as sumptuous, while St Margaret's has a unique design of roof.

The major Presbyterian denominations favoured large steepled Gothic Revival churches. The oldest is Meadowside St Paul's (formerly St Paul's Free, 1852, **50**), for the Church of Scotland. It was followed by a series of churches along the Perth Road, a middle-class enclave. The former St John's (Free, 1884), now West, was the first, then the former St Mark's Church of Scotland (1868–9) and finally the former McCheyne Memorial (Free, 1870). The two latter are by F. W. Pilkington, whose interpretation of the Gothic Revival was idiosyncratic. All three parishes have been united as Dundee West, worshipping in the renamed St John's. To the north of the town centre are

Fig. 20. St Columba's Roman Catholic Church, Kirkton, City of Dundee

Fig. 21. Chalmers Ardler Parish Church, City of Dundee

Stobswell (originally Ogilvie Free, 1874, **59**) and Balgay (1902, **49**). Of the former United Presbyterian churches, a striking example is the former Victoria Street (1875, Fig. 17). St John's Cross Church of Scotland (1911–14), now Logie and St John's Cross, is a massive Romanesque Revival building in the west end. One of the most unusual Dundee churches is the Gilfillan Memorial (1887, Fig. 18), built by a congregation which broke away from the United Presbyterian Church, as part of a commercial and residential development. Its frontage is confidently Baroque, a rare style in Scotland.

Few churches were built in Dundee between the wars. The Craigie estate, a model for its time, was provided with a neat little Scottish Episcopal church, St Ninian's (1938); and a large stripped Romanesque church was built at Mid Craigie (1937, now closed). The churches built to serve the post-Second World War municipal housing estates were in a range of styles. Seven were constructed for the Roman Catholic Church, and five for the Church of Scotland. The earliest were St Vincent de Paul's Roman Catholic Church, Kingsway East (1950) and Mains of Fintry Church of Scotland (1954), and the last was the Roman Catholic Church of St Leonard and St Fergus, Ardler (1975). The earlier ones were in modern variations of traditional styles; later ones were more clearly modernist. Examples of the former include Menzieshill Church of Scotland (1962, Fig. 19) and the Roman Catholic church of St Columba, Kirkton (1963, Fig. 20), and of the latter Chalmers Ardler Church of Scotland (1968, Fig. 21).

As indicated above, Broughty Ferry is essentially a middle-class suburb of Dundee, and as such had a full complement of large, confident church buildings. Of the Presbyterian denominations, there are St Stephen's and West (1871–80, formerly St Stephen's Church of Scotland), a large Gothic Revival building with ornamental slating; St James's (1889), a Romanesque building; St Luke's and Queen Street (1884, formerly St Luke's); and Broughty Ferry New (1824,

Fig. 22. The former Blackford Old Parish Church, Perth & Kinross

formerly St Aidan's). There are also a large Scottish Episcopal church (St Mary's, 1858–70 and 1911, **44**) and the brick Roman Catholic Our Lady of Good Counsel (1904, **45**).

Perth and Kinross

The extent and quality of the early Christian sculpture and of the remains of medieval churches in this area strongly suggest that its agriculture was, by the standards of the time, relatively prosperous. Even before agricultural improvement became general across lowland Scotland, it seems that farming in Perthshire, Kinross-shire and Angus was becoming more productive. Trade with northern Europe through the ports of Perth, Dundee, Arbroath and Montrose stimulated the local economy, and from the 1720s the making of linen cloth, largely from flax imported from the Baltic, complemented agriculture. Sculpture on tombstones in, for instance, Abernyte churchyard shows handlooms and shuttles. The construction of Orwell, Milnathort (1729, **104**), the first part of Abernyte (1736, **62**), Blackford Old (1738–9, Fig. 22) and even Amulree (1743, **66**) churches may well reflect prosperity based on linen manufacture and better farming.

Later in the eighteenth century, improved roads enlivened rural economies, and this probably stimulated church-building, where new roads made it easier for farmers to travel to church. Kettins (1768, **96**), Trinity Gask (c. 1770), Aberdalgie (1773, **60**) and Forteviot (1778, **88**) are all churches of this character, though Kettins and Aberdalgie have since been significantly altered. Kenmore (1760) is quite different, an estate church designed (possibly by an English architect) as the focal point of its village, with a tower on its front gable. These are all Church of Scotland buildings – but, from the 1730s, especially in rural areas, groups split from the Established Church over the issue of state involvement in Church affairs. The first Secession, of 1734, was followed by a split over the requirement for men living in burghs to accept that the Established Church was theologically justified. Thereafter, until 1820, there were two strands within Secessionism: Burghers and Antiburghers. There were subsequently further splits, which need not concern

Fig. 23. The former Kinkell Church of Scotland (ex-Antiburgher Secession), Perth & Kinross

Fig. 24. Abernethy and Dron Parish Church (St Bride's), Perth & Kinross

us here. Perth and Kinross were strongholds of Secessionism, one of the earliest Secession churches being the 'Kirk o' the Muir' near Murthly (1743), hidden up a farm track, and now a ruin. Later Secession churches include three, in Greenloaning, Broom of Dalreoch and Kinkell (c. 1790, Fig. 23), now converted into houses. Kilmaveonaig, near Blair Atholl (1794, **97**), is an early rural Scottish Episcopal church in an isolated location.

It was in the 1780s that the Scottish economy really began to expand, and with it church-building. The French wars of the 1790s, and later, resulted in high prices for farm produce, especially grain, favouring areas like central Perthshire. Among the new churches built from the 1780s are Ardoch (1780–1, **67**), Dunbarney (1787, **84**), Little Dunkeld (1797–8, **101**), Gask (1800, **91**), Abernethy (1801–2, Fig. 24), Glendevon (1803, **92**), a remodelling of a seventeenth-century building, and Scone Old (1806, **121**). All of these are low, long buildings except Abernethy, which is tall and broad with a horseshoe gallery. The body of Longforgan (1795, **102**) is also tall and broad, though its arrangement of windows is different. Caputh (1798 and later, **75**) is also of this period, but has been much altered. Abernethy and Longforgan have pointed 'Gothick' windows, heralding the arrival of the early Gothic Revival in Perthshire. The former St Paul's, Perth (1806–7, Fig. 25) is a very early example of a large Gothic Revival church, a hybrid, with its octagonal plan and steeple. The old church of Comrie (1805), now a hall, has pointed windows and a classical steeple.

Within a very few years, the tall rectangular Gothic church with a pinnacled tower had emerged as a distinct type. Collace (1812–13, **78**) was one of the first, followed by Muthill (1826, **106**), Errol (1831) and, in modified form, Stanley (1828, **124**), a cotton-mill village

Fig. 25. The former St Paul's Parish Church, Perth, Perth & Kinross

church, and Clunie (1839–40, Fig. 26). Kinnaird (1815, **99**) and St Anne's, Dowally (1818, **83**) are smaller, simpler Gothic churches. Foss (1824, **89**), also small and simple, has the square-headed windows fashionable in the mid-eighteenth century. Large, elaborate early Gothic Revival churches are to be found at Kinnoull, Perth (1827, **111**) and Inchture (1834–5, **93**). These buildings were all constructed for the established Church of Scotland. In 1825–6, Methven and Logiealmond Parish Church (originally constructed in 1782–3) was enlarged and remodelled, with a classical steeple. Apart from Comrie Old Parish Church (see above), this is the only steeple of the type in Perthshire.

In the later 1820s, new 'Parliamentary' parishes (with standard churches and manses), on the recommendation of Thomas Telford, were carved out of old ones to meet the needs of growing Highland populations. Though none of these was in Perthshire, two churches in Highland Perthshire were built on the Telford/Thomson model. Innerwick, Glenlyon (1828, Fig. 27) was originally virtually identical to the standard church; and the Old Church of Rannoch, Kinloch Rannoch (1829, **122**) contains features, such as window frames, like the standard churches. These churches have 'Tudor' windows, with flattened arched heads, which became popular briefly in the 1830s. The Kinross-shire churches of Cleish (1832, **77**) and Kinross (1831–2, **100**) are in a variant of this style, with battlemented towers. Little Tenandry (1836, **126**) and Portmoak (1832, **120**) have windows of this type, as does the elegant church of Monzie (1830–1, Fig. 28). The most elaborate church in this style in Perthshire is probably St Martin's (1843), with a magnificent Gothic canopied pulpit.

By that time, Perthshire was becoming more religiously and culturally diverse. Early Scottish Episcopal churches were built in Muthill (St James's, 1836, **107**) and Blairgowrie (St Catharine's, 1842–3, **73**); and what appears to have been the first Roman Catholic church in the area was constructed in Perth (St John the Baptist, 1832 on, **110**). These were all fashionably, if modestly, Gothic. Uniquely exuberant is the Roman Catholic private chapel of St Anthony the Eremite, Murthly Castle (1845–6). In contrast, the former St Leonard's, a 'chapel of ease' in Perth, was daringly and strikingly classical (1834–6,

Fig. 26. Clunie Parish Church, Perth & Kinross

Fig. 27. Glenlyon Parish Church, Innerwick, Perth & Kinross

Fig. 29). It remained an isolated example. Another church that 'broke the mould' is Alyth Parish Church (1839, **64**), which in massing is an early steepled Gothic Revival church, but in detail is a good example of the first Romanesque revival in Scotland.

In the 1840s, two developments took place which had a profound effect on Perthshire. The first was the 1843 Disruption, which split the Church of Scotland over a number of issues, notably the right of landowners to appoint ministers. Those who left the Established Church formed the Free Church. The second development, at the end of the decade, was the construction of railways. Perth became a node in the Scottish railway system, reinforcing its role as a regional centre. That role continued to grow in the second half of the nineteenth century. Railways encouraged the growth of industry and also agricultural specialisation. The resulting prosperity resulted in sporadic, but significant, church-building between 1850 and 1914. Early Free churches included Aberfeldy (now Church of Scotland, 1843, **61**), the delightful little Glenfincastle Chapel (1843–4, Fig. 30), and what is now Cargill Burrelton Parish Church (1854–5, **76**). A later, unusual building is Scone New Parish Church (formerly Scone Free, 1886–7), dominated by a steeply crow-stepped saddle-back tower.

Episcopalianism flourished in mid-nineteenth-century Perthshire. The most striking evidence of this was the founding of St Ninian's Cathedral in Perth in 1850 (**109**). It took many years for it to reach its present form, but this early intention is striking. The second Scottish Episcopal church in Perth is St John's (1850–1, **114**), like St Ninian's in an advanced Gothic Revival style, the most sophisticated yet seen in the area. These were followed in the late 1850s by St Mary's, Birnam (1858, **71**) and Holy Trinity, Pitlochry

Fig. 28. Monzie Parish Church, Perth & Kinross

(1858, **118**), both modest 'village churches' probably built for rail-borne visitors from England; by that time, the Scottish Episcopal Church had explicitly aligned itself with the Church of England.

The largest and finest churches built in Perth during the later nineteenth century were constructed for the Free and United Presbyterian churches. The latter had been formed in 1847 by a union between the successors of the original eighteenth-century Secession churches. It was largely a middle-class, urban church. The first of these large churches was the West Free (now St Matthew's Parish Church, 1869–71, **116**), a striking feature of the Perth waterfront. Next was the North United Presbyterian Church (now North Church, 1878–80, **112**), in Italian Romanesque. The last was what is now St Leonard's-in-the-Fields (fomerly St Leonard's Free Church, 1882–5, **113**), in old Scots Gothic style, on a splendid site facing the open South Inch, a public park. There are also smaller Gothic Methodist (1879) and Congregational (1897–8) churches in Perth. The popularity of Perthshire as a holiday destination led to the construction of large new churches in Comrie (Free, 1879–81, **79**, now the Church of Scotland parish church), Crieff (Church of Scotland, 1880–2, **81**; and the former United Presbyterian Church, 1883–4, now St Andrew's Halls) and Pitlochry (1884, **117**). All of these are Gothic except the Pitlochry church, which is in an eclectic Romanesque style.

In the country, the Scottish Episcopal Church continued to gain ground, probably because many upper middle-class men from the central belt bought small country estates in Perthshire in the late nineteenth century. St David's, Weem (1878, **128**, now the parish church), St Andrew's, Strathtay (1888, **125**) and St Michael's, Ballintuim (1899, **70**) are all small country churches. St Columba's, Stanley (1898) is a mission church built as a prefabricated structure by Speirs & Co. of Glasgow. The striking half-timbered All Saints, Glencarse (1878) and St Kessog's, Auchterarder (1897, **68**) are larger, as is All Souls', Invergowrie (1890–6, **95**). Invergowrie is close to Dundee, and had until the 1960s a large paper mill. It got a large Church of Scotland church in 1906–9 (**94**). Both of the Invergowrie churches are Gothic Revival, as is the present Blairgowrie Parish Church (1904, **72**). This was built by the United Free Church, formed in 1900 as a union between the Free and United Presbyterian churches. Another

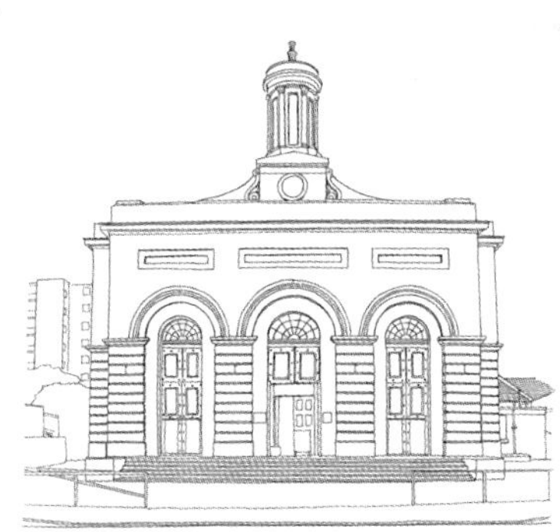

Fig. 29. The former St Leonard's Parish Church, Perth

Fig. 30. Glenfincastle Chapel (ex-Free), Perth & Kinross

United Free church is what is now Dunning Church (1908–9, **87**), a small Gothic building. The Church of Scotland built few new country churches in the Victorian period, among them Kinclaven (1848, **98**), Meigle (1870, **103**) and Dundurn, St Fillan's (1878, **85**).

In the first decade of the twentieth century, there was a short-lived vogue for 'Arts and Crafts' design in central Perthshire. Sir Donald Currie, a noted ship-owner, rebuilt the village of Fortingall in English Arts and Crafts style. The church (1901–2, Fig. 31) is, however, in Scots Gothic style, with an Arts and Crafts flavour. Currie also paid for the 'restoration' of the choir of Dunkeld Cathedral (**86**), with magnificent Scots Gothic furnishings. Auchterarder Parish Church (1904–5) is mildly Art Nouveau, though most of its original furnishings have recently been removed. The other Arts and Crafts churches in Perthshire are Braes of Rannoch (1907, **74**), an early Christian design by Peter Macgregor Chalmers, and Morenish Chapel, near Killin (1902, **105**), designed as a memorial to the daughter of a local landowning family. Traces of Arts and Crafts thinking lingered on into the 1920s, when the medieval St John's Kirk, Perth was restored and adapted by Sir Robert Lorimer (1923–6, **108**) as a memorial to Perth people who had died in the First World War.

Unlike many other 'lowland' parts of Scotland, there was little development of new housing areas after either World War. The exception is Perth, where new housing was built round the old core after the Second World War, with some new churches. In Craigie, to the south, there are two churches: St Mary Magdalene Roman Catholic Church (1958–9, **115**) and Craigend-Moncrieffe (1951, 1974–5); in Muirton, to the north, is Riverside (2002); and in Letham are a Mormon church (1969), the Roman Catholic church of Our Lady of Lourdes (1958–9) and a recent Church of Scotland, replacing a Church Extension building of the

Fig. 31. Fortingall Parish Church, Perth & Kinross

1950s. Finally, in Tulloch, there is a new Free church (1989). A rare example of a modern country church is Aberuthven (1991, **63**), simply functional. The latest church in Perth and Kinross is Auchtergaven and Moneydie Parish Church (**69**), in the village of Bankfoot, completed in 2008 as an 'eco-church' to replace the former Auchtergaven Parish Church. This sat on top of a hill above the village, and was destroyed by fire in 2004. Rather than rebuild it on its inaccessible and cramped site, the congregation decided to build on a new site in the village.

Conclusion

The area covered in this volume does not, generally speaking, have an obvious sacredness as do, for instance, places like Iona, Whithorn or Orkney. It is, by and large, a settled area with the stability which comes from arable farming and large landed estates. But, within this settled place, there are many buildings and artefacts that are evidence of places of spiritual meaning, worthy of pilgrimage. The enigmatic Pictish stones; the relics of pre-Roman Christianity; the places where the Victorians sought to provide worthy edifices to hear the Word and to celebrate the Eucharist; the buildings put up by those who found 'official' religion too stifling – all of these and many more are worth thinking about and experiencing. And all of these buildings and objects are set in landscapes and townscapes as fine as any that can be found in Scotland: the broad valleys of Strathmore, Strathtay and Strathearn, the tidal basin of Montrose and the Arbroath cliffs all have qualities of spaciousness and calm which lead to contemplation. The Highland landscapes of the Perthshire and Angus glens have that edginess which stimulates thought about the differences between Highland and Lowland people. And in the villages, towns and city, there is ample evidence of the love of people for place, of sharing experience and humanity that is inherent in the Scottish approach to life, crystallised in the places of worship, sacred in so many ways, haunted by memories of faithful people over so many generations.

PROFESSOR JOHN R. HUME
Universities of Glasgow and St Andrews

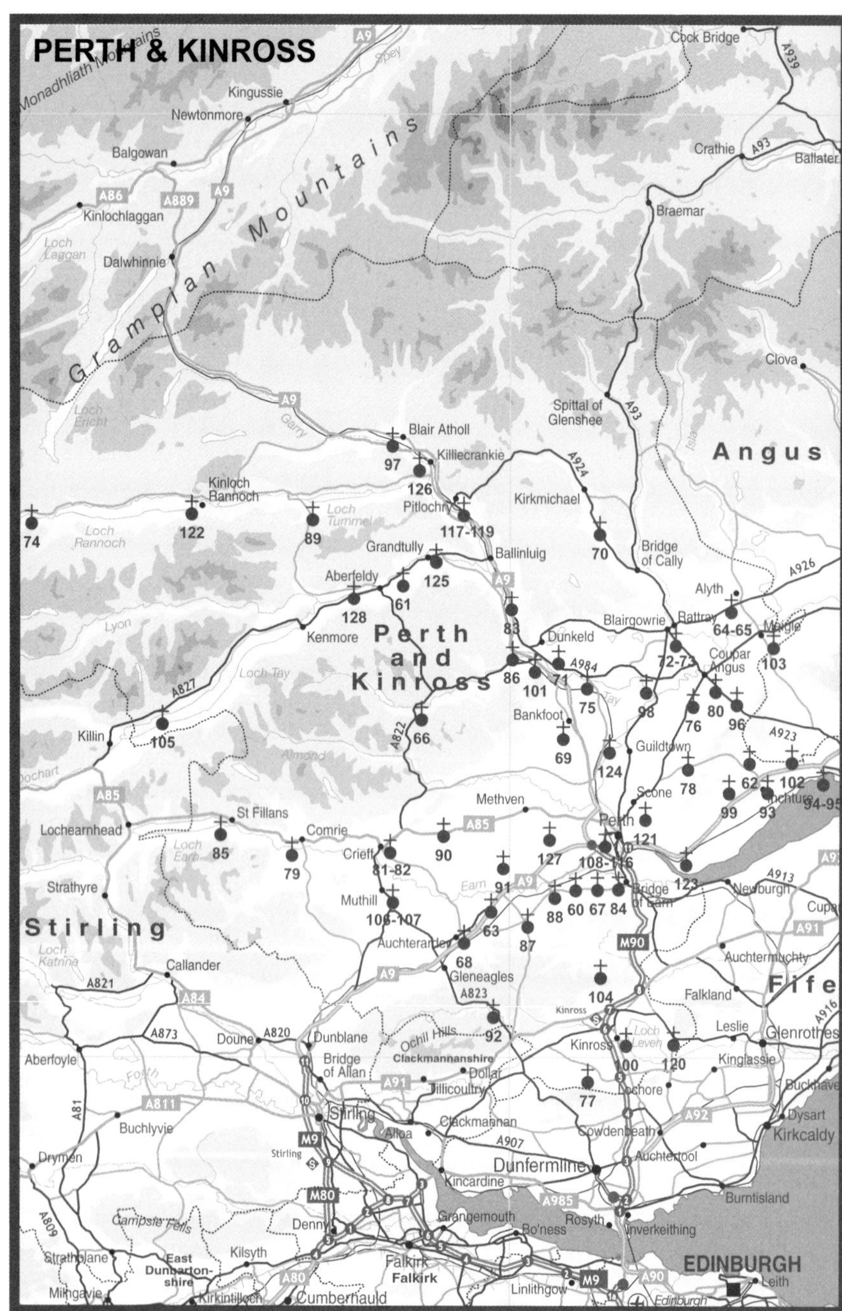
PERTH & KINROSS
Grampian Mountains
Angus
Perth and Kinross
Stirling
Fife
Kingussie
Newtonmore
Balgowan
Kinlochlaggan
Dalwhinnie
Cock Bridge
Crathie
Ballater
Braemar
Clova
Spittal of Glenshee
Blair Atholl
Killiecrankie
Kinloch Rannoch
Loch Rannoch
Loch Tummel
Pitlochry
Kirkmichael
Grandtully
Ballinluig
Bridge of Cally
Aberfeldy
Kenmore
Alyth
Blairgowrie
Rattray
Dunkeld
Coupar Angus
Meigle
Loch Tay
Bankfoot
Guildtown
Killin
Methven
Scone
Perth
Inchture
Lochearnhead
St Fillans
Comrie
Crieff
Loch Earn
Strathyre
Muthill
Bridge of Earn
Newburgh
Auchterarder
Gleneagles
Auchtermuchty
Callander
Falkland
Kinross
Loch Leven
Leslie
Glenrothes
Aberfoyle
Doune
Dunblane
Bridge of Allan
Ochil Hills
Clackmannanshire
Dollar
Tillicoultry
Kinglassie
Lochore
Buchlyvie
Stirling
Alloa
Clackmannan
Cowdenbeath
Dysart
Kirkcaldy
Drymen
Auchtertool
Dunfermline
Kincardine
Burntisland
Campsie Fells
Denny
Grangemouth
Bo'ness
Rosyth
Inverkeithing
Strathblane
East Dunbartonshire
Kilsyth
Falkirk
Linlithgow
EDINBURGH
Leith
Milngavie
Kirkintilloch
Cumbernauld
A9
A86
A889
A93
A939
A924
A926
A827
A822
A984
A923
A85
A913
A91
A821
A84
A873
A820
A823
A811
A81
A907
A92
A985
A809
A80
A90
M90
M9
M80
74
122
89
97
126
117-119
70
125
61
128
83
64-65
103
72-73
86
101
71
75
98
76
80
96
105
66
69
124
78
62
102
94-95
99
93
85
90
127
121
108-116
79
81-82
91
88
60
67
84
123
106-107
63
87
68
104
92
100
120
77

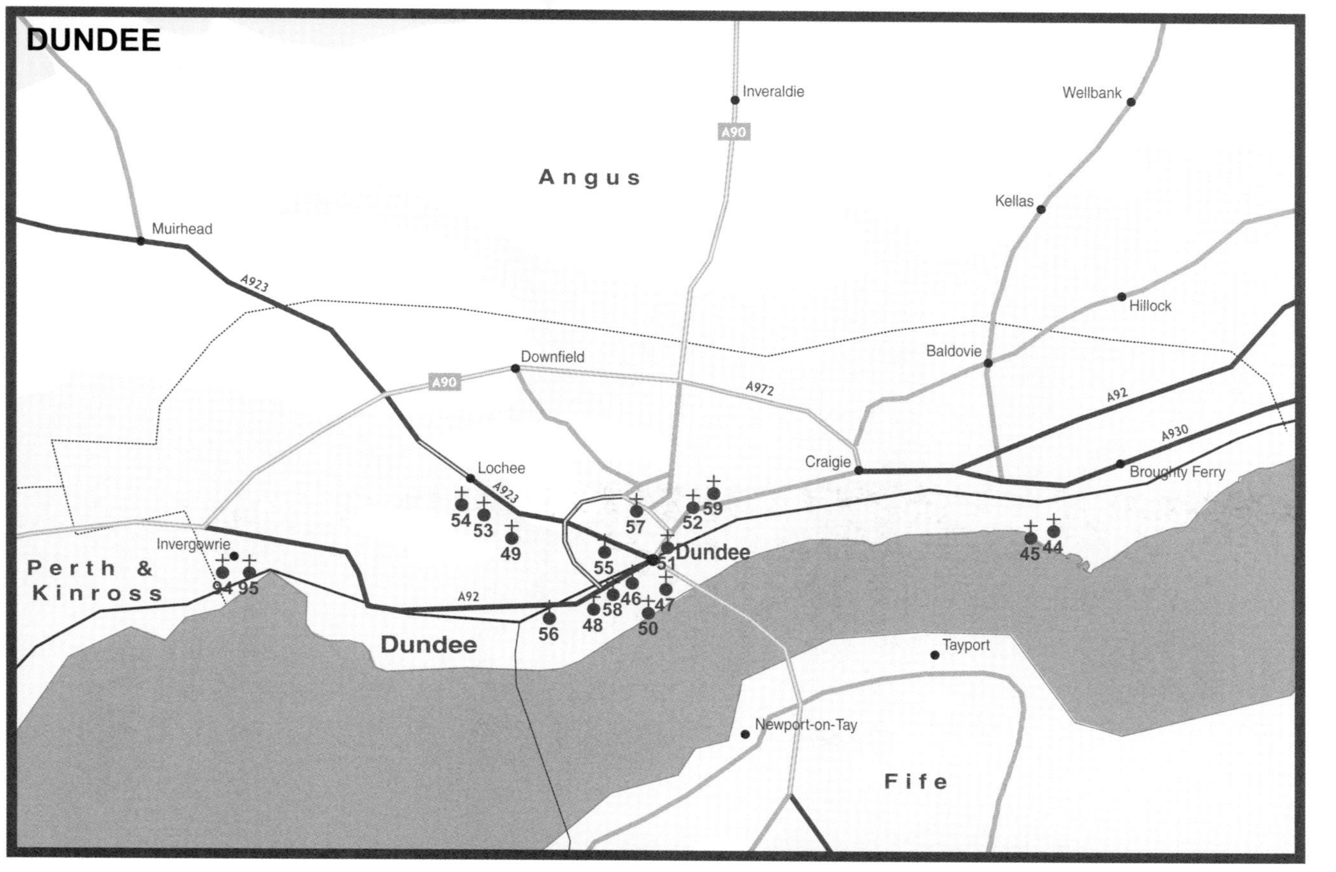
DUNDEE
Inveraldie
Wellbank
A90
Angus
Kellas
Muirhead
A923
Hillock
Baldovie
Downfield
A90
A972
A92
A930
Craigie
Broughty Ferry
Lochee
A923
54
53
49
57
52
59
45
44
Invergowrie
Dundee
51
55
46
58
47
48
50
56
Perth &
Kinross
94
95
A92
Dundee
Tayport
Newport-on-Tay
Fife

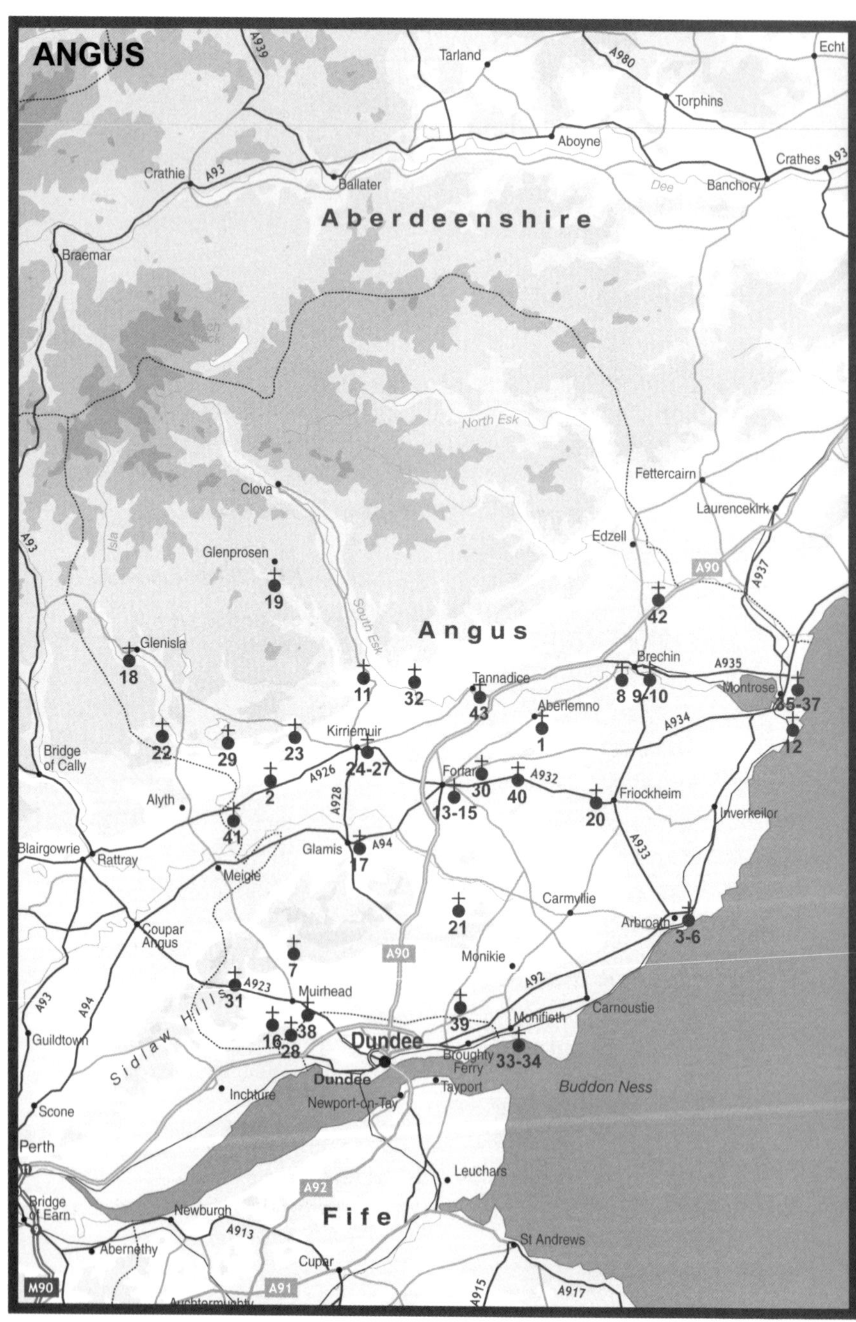

ANGUS
Aberdeenshire
Angus
Fife
Tarland
Echt
Torphins
Aboyne
Crathes
Banchory
Dee
Crathie
Ballater
Braemar
North Esk
Fettercairn
Laurencekirk
Edzell
Clova
Glenprosen
South Esk
Isla
Glenisla
Brechin
Montrose
Tannadice
Aberlemno
Kirriemuir
Bridge of Cally
Forfar
Friockheim
Inverkeilor
Alyth
Blairgowrie
Rattray
Glamis
Meigle
Carmyllie
Arbroath
Coupar Angus
Monikie
Muirhead
Carnoustie
Monifieth
Sidlaw Hills
Guildtown
Dundee
Broughty Ferry
Tayport
Buddon Ness
Inchture
Newport-on-Tay
Scone
Perth
Leuchars
Bridge of Earn
Newburgh
Abernethy
St Andrews
Cupar
Auchtermuchty
A939
A980
A93
A90
A937
A935
A934
A932
A926
A928
A94
A933
A923
A92
A913
A91
A915
A917
M90
1
2
3-6
7
8
9-10
11
12
13-15
16
17
18
19
20
21
22
23
24-27
28
29
30
31
32
33-34
35-37
38
39
40
41
42
43

How to use this Guide

Entries are arranged by local-authority area, with large areas sub-divided for convenience. The number preceding each entry refers to the map. Each entry is followed by symbols for access and facilities:

- Ordnance Survey reference
- Denomination
- Church website
- ● Regular services
- ○ Church events
- ● Opening arrangements
- Wheelchair access for partially abled
- WC Toilets available for visitors
- WC Toilets adapted for the disabled available for visitors
- Hearing induction loop for the deaf
- Welcomers and guides on duty
- Guidebooks and souvenirs available/for sale
- NADFAS Church Recorders' Inventory (NADFAS)
- Refreshments
- A Category A listing
- B Category B listing
- C Category C listing

Category A: Buildings of national or international importance, either architectural or historic, or fine little-altered examples of some particular period, style or building type.

Category B: Buildings of regional or more than local importance, or major examples of some particular period, style or building type which may have been altered.

Category C: Buildings of local importance, lesser examples of any period, style, or building type, as originally constructed or moderately altered; and simple traditional buildings which group well with others in categories A and B.

The information appearing in the gazetteer of this guide is supplied by the participating churches. While this is believed to be correct at the time of going to press, Scotland's Churches Scheme cannot accept any responsibility for its accuracy.

1 ABERLEMNO PARISH CHURCH

Aberlemno
DD8 3PE

NO 523 555

Church of Scotland

Linked with Guthrie (20), Rescobie (40)

8km (5 miles) east of Forfar on B9134

Small oblong church rebuilt in 1722 on site of pre-Reformation church. Extended to a T-plan in 1820 and remodelled in Gothic style in the late 19th century. Vestry and galleries added in 1856. Famous 8th-century standing stone in kirkyard (covered in winter months). Pre-Reformation stone font was brought into the church in 1992.

- Sunday: 10.00am or 11.30am (times change monthly; please contact minister for details)
- Open during daylight hours (01241 828243)

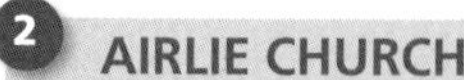

2 AIRLIE CHURCH

Kirkton of Airlie
DD8 5NL

NO 313 515

Church of Scotland

Linked with Glenisla (18), Kilry (22), Kingoldrum (23), Lintrathen (29), Ruthven (41)

1.6km (1 mile) north of A926

Stands on a site where the Gospel has been preached for over 780 years. The present simple building was completed in 1783. The interior was renovated in 1893 using pitch-pine, and an extension added to accommodate the pipe organ and choir. Pre-Reformation relics. The oldest gravestone is dated 1609.

- Sunday: 6.30pm in rotation with Glenisla, Kingoldrum, Lintrathen and Ruthven
- Open by arrangement (01575 560260)

3 ST ANDREW'S PARISH CHURCH, ARBROATH

**Hamilton Green
Arbroath
DD11 1JG**

NO 644 412

Church of Scotland

www.arbroathstandrews.org.uk/

Opposite Arbroath Abbey Visitor Centre

On first impressions, entirely typical of its time, having been built in the late 1880s. However, following extensive refurbishment in 2009, it now stands as a brilliant example of new inside old. Beautifully appointed, with striking decoration, the combination of traditional and contemporary is well worth a visit.

- Sunday: 11.00am; Wednesday: 10.30am
- Open weekday mornings 9.00am–12.30pm (01241 431135)

ST VIGEANS CHURCH, ARBROATH

**St Vigeans
Arbroath
DD11 4RD**

NO 639 429

Church of Scotland

www.stvigeanschurch.org

Red sandstone church on a smooth green mound. Dedicated to St Vigean (or Fechin), Irish saint, who died AD 664. Church rebuilt in 12th century, but not dedicated until 1242. Some 15th-century alterations, then a major restoration in the 19th century by Robert Rowand Anderson. Largely unaltered since. Lovely stained-glass windows. Organ by Harrison, 1875. Nearby St Vigeans Museum has collection of spectacular Pictish stones.

- Sunday: 11.30am
- Open by arrangement (01241 873206)

5 ST THOMAS OF CANTERBURY, ARBROATH

**Dishlandtown Street
Arbroath
DD11 1QU**

NO 638 406

Roman Catholic

Church opened for worship in 1848, designed by George Mathewson of Dundee. Romanesque design with aisled nave and chancel. The front is a miniature replica of St Augustine's gateway at Canterbury. Unique 1-manual and pedal organ by Postill of York, c. 1860, now rebuilt.

- Saturday: 6.30pm; Sunday: 10.30am
- Open daily 9.00am–6.00pm (01241 873013)

6 ST JOHN'S, ARBROATH

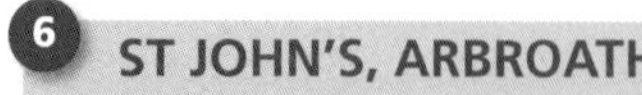

'Totum Kirkie'

**15 Ponderlaw Street
Arbroath
DD11 1EU**

NO 645 411

Methodist

Opened for worship by Rev. John Wesley on 6 May 1772. Built in the octagonal style favoured by Wesley, this is the only one of these churches left in Scotland. Known as the 'Totum Kirkie'. Remodelled, and porch and vestibule added, 1883. The Lifeboat Window is a memorial to the loss of the lifeboat *Robert L. Lindsay* and six crew members in 1953. Old manse adjacent to church.

- Sunday: 11.00am
- Open by arrangement (01674 672373)

7 AUCHTERHOUSE PARISH CHURCH

Kirkton of Auchterhouse
DD3 0QT

NO 342 381

Church of Scotland

www.sidlawchurches.com/pages/worship/1.php

Linked with Murroes & Tealing (39)

1.6km (1 mile) east of B954

Built 1630 with stone from earlier churches of 1275 and 1426. Partially rebuilt, 1775. Chancel and nave with tower at west end. Burial vault at east end. Interior completely renovated, 1910. Gothic chancel arch lends character and dignity. Three impressive stained-glass windows, medieval octagonal font, stool of repentance and 18th-century clock.

- Sunday: 11.00am on 1st and 3rd Sunday of the month, 9.30am on 2nd and 4th Sunday
- Open by arrangement (01382 456838)

8 BENHOLM KIRK

Benholm
DD10 0HT

NO 804 693

Former Church of Scotland

www.srct.org.uk

In centre of village, 1.6km (1 mile) north of Johnshaven, off A92

Externally plain, slated and harled Georgian rural parish kirk of 1832, incorporating 15th-century sacrament house and 17th-century monuments of national significance from earlier church. Notable are the 1620 monument to Lady Mary Keith, a fusion of Renaissance architectural details and traditional symbolism and the much more sophisticated 1690 Scott Monument in white marble with cherubs, drapery and foliage. Church transferred to ownership of Scottish Redundant Churches Trust in 2006.

- Occasional services: see website
- Open daily 9.00am–6.00pm (01334 472032)

9 BRECHIN CATHEDRAL

**Church Lane
Brechin
DD9 6JS**

NO 595 601

Church of Scotland

www.brechincathedral.org.uk

Linked with Stracathro (42)

Founded 11th century; round tower of that date is of Irish inspiration. Church contains 13th-, 14th- and 15th-century medieval architecture. Major restoration in 1900–2 supervised by J. Honeyman (Honeyman, Keppie & Mackintosh). Special features include 12th-century font and a collection of Pictish sculptures. Stunning 20th-century stained glass.

- Sunday: 10.30am; 9.30am on 2nd Sunday of the month at Stracathro Church
- Open most days all year, 9.00am–4.30pm and by arrangement (01356 629360) (Monday to Friday 10.00am–12.00 noon)

   (in halls)  

 (by arrangement)

10 ST NINIAN'S CHURCH, BRECHIN

**Bank Street
Brechin
DD9 7AH**

NO 600 603

Roman Catholic

Linked with St Margaret's, Montrose (36)

Tall, simple church of 1875 in Normandy Gothic, distinctive of the architect William Leiper. Small octagonal spire on the left of the front gable. Interior enlivened by stained glass and murals.

- Sunday: 10.00am; Tuesday and Thursday: 10.00am
- Open by arrangement (01674 672208)

11 CORTACHY CHURCH

Cortachy
DD8 4QF

NO 396 597

Church of Scotland

www.gkopc.co.uk

Linked with Glen Prosen (19), Kirriemuir Old (24), Memus (32)

At gates of Cortachy Castle, off B955

Built by the 7th Earl of Airlie, the sole heritor, in 1828 on the site of a previous church. The architect was David Patterson. Magnificent setting overlooking the River South Esk. Inside, there are memorials to the 9th and 12th Earls, and against the east gable is the burial aisle of the Airlie family.

- Sunday: 10.00am
- Open by arrangement (01575 572819)

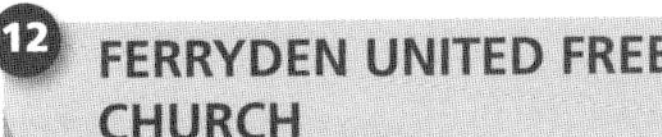

12 FERRYDEN UNITED FREE CHURCH

Bellevue Terrace
Ferryden
DD10 9RG

NO 718 567

United Free Church

Linked with Knox UFC, Montrose (37)

East end of village

A small building, accommodating 70, the church was opened in 1935 to meet the needs of families from the fishing community who did not adhere to the 1929 union of churches. An annual sea service continues to be held on the second Sunday in November.

- Sunday: 6.00pm
- Open by arrangement (01674 673772)

13 LOWSON MEMORIAL PARISH CHURCH, FORFAR

Jameson Street
Forfar
DD8 2HY

NO 465 509

Church of Scotland

http://lowsonchurch.org

East end of Forfar, off Montrose Road

A gem of a church designed by A. Marshall Mackenzie, 1914, in the style of late Scots Gothic, cruciform in shape with five-bay nave, aisleless transepts, one-bay chancel and central tower with spire. Built of a ruddy-hued local stone. Excellent stained glass, including windows by Douglas Strachan.

- Sunday: 11.00am
- Open Monday to Friday 9.30am–4.30pm all year (01307 463931)

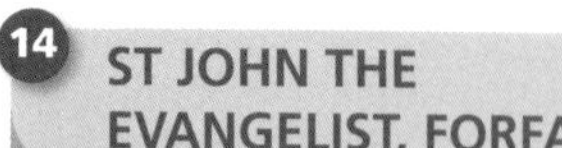

14 ST JOHN THE EVANGELIST, FORFAR

71 East High Street
Forfar
DD8 2EP

NO 458 507

Scottish Episcopal

www.stjohnsforfar.co.uk

Linked with St Mary's, Kirriemuir (25), St Margaret's, Lunanhead (30)

Built on the site of an earlier church, the present building was designed in Early English style by Sir Robert Rowand Anderson and consecrated in 1881. The font has traditionally been associated with St Margaret and Restenneth Priory. 3-manual pipe organ by Conacher of Huddersfield. Stained glass by Charles E. Kempe and Septimus Waugh. Historic graveyard pre-dates present church.

- Sunday: 8.30am and 11.00am; weekdays: as announced
- Open daily, summer months 9.00am–4.00pm, winter months 9.00am–2.00pm (01307 463440)

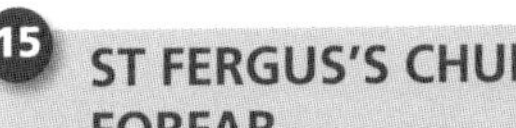

15 ST FERGUS'S CHURCH, FORFAR

96 Glenogil Terrace
Forfar
DD8 1NG

NO 453 498

Roman Catholic

Linked with St Anthony's, Kirriemuir (27)

Opened in 1963 to replace original 1946 parish church on the High Street. Stations of the Cross designed by local artist William Cadenhead. Patron St Fergus was an 8th-century bishop who travelled across the east of Scotland.

- Sunday: 11.00am
- Open by arrangement (01307 462104)

16 ST MARNOCK'S CHURCH, FOWLIS EASTER

Fowlis Easter
DD2 5SB

NO 322 334

Church of Scotland

Linked with Liff (28), Lundie (31), Muirhead (38)

In centre of Fowlis Easter, 1.6km (1 mile) west of Liff

Constructed in 1453 and notable for the oak board paintings of the Crucifixion and of saints dating from the same period, and rood screen doors from the 15th century. Stained glass commemorates the Gray family which founded this collegiate church. Cross-slab gravestone in graveyard.

- Sunday: 10.00am in January, February, May, August, September, November and December
- Open by arrangement (01382 580210)

ST FERGUS'S CHURCH, GLAMIS

Glamis Parish Church

Kirk Wynd
Glamis
DD8 1RT

NO 386 469

Church of Scotland

www.stferguskirkglamis.co.uk/welcome.html

Linked with Inverarity (21)

Close to Angus Folk Museum

Present church built 1792 on site of church dedicated to St Fergus, 1242. Substantially altered and beautified, 1933. Classical bell-tower with octagonal top stage and spire. Kirkyard with interesting stones. Strathmore Aisle built 1459 by Isabella Ogilvy on death of her husband Patrick Lyon, 1st Lord Glamis. 7th-century Celtic stone in garden of former manse, opposite the church.

- Sunday: 11.30am
- Open by arrangement (01307 840488)

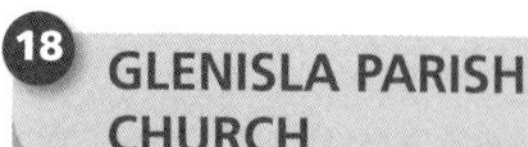

GLENISLA PARISH CHURCH

Glenisla
PH11 8PH

NO 215 604

Church of Scotland

Linked with Airlie (2), Kilry (22), Kingoldrum (23), Lintrathen (29), Ruthven (41)

B951, head of Glenisla

Lovely rural setting at the head of Glenisla. Small oblong Gothic building with belfry of 1821. Attached hearse-house on north wall, of later date. Church remodelled internally c. 1952. Session house.

- Sunday: 6.30pm in rotation with Airlie, Kingoldrum, Lintrathen and Ruthven
- Open by arrangement (01575 500267)

19 GLEN PROSEN CHURCH

Glenprosen Village
DD8 4SA

NO 328 657

Church of Scotland

www.gkopc.co.uk

Linked with Cortachy (11), Kirriemuir Old (24), Memus (32)

Head of Glen Prosen

Present church built 1801–2, paid for by local inhabitants, ensuring continuous worship in the glen for nearly 400 years. It is a simple, traditional whitewashed church. Special features include wood carvings by Sir Robert Lorimer and war-memorial porch with rare slated cross. The Minister's Road leads from here to Glen Clova, so named because the minister used to walk it twice each Sunday.

- Sunday: 12.00 noon on 1st and 3rd Sunday of the month; 6.00pm April to September, 1st Sunday of the month
- Open daily, access via vestry door (01575 572819)

B

20 GUTHRIE PARISH CHURCH

Guthrie
DD8 2TP

NO 568 505

Church of Scotland

Linked with Aberlemno (1), Rescobie (40)

800 metres (½ mile) north of A932, 11km (7 miles) east of Forfar

Present church was built in 1826 to a Telford design. The 15th-century Guthrie Aisle is beside the church. Two stained-glass windows: 'The Good Shepherd' (1920), Dickson family; and 'The Sower' (1976), Guthries of California.

- Sunday: 10.00am or 11.30am or 6.30pm (times change monthly; please contact minister for details)
- Open at all times (01241 828243)

21 INVERARITY PARISH CHURCH

Inverarity
DD8 2JU

NO 460 440

Church of Scotland

www.stferguskirkglamis.co.uk/welcome.html

Linked with Glamis (17)

Eastern side of village on B9217

Church built 1754, with recent impressive renovation. White-harled traditional church with round-headed windows. Kirk bell by Peter van der Ghein dated 1614, cast in Holland. Gable porches added, 1854. Stained-glass window (1997) of three geese by Aileen Ogilvie and based on an original picture by Barbara Robertson. Modern church/community hall next to church.

- Sunday: 10.00am
- Open by arrangement (01307 840488)

22 KILRY PARISH CHURCH

Dykehead
PH11 8HU

NO 246 538

Church of Scotland

Linked with Airlie (2), Glenisla (18), Kingoldrum (23), Lintrathen (29), Ruthven (41)

6.5km (4 miles) north of Alyth

Stands in a valley on the edge of the hills at the entrance to Glenisla. Small, oblong, Gothic, harled kirk, 1876–7, with belfry and session house.

- Sunday: 10.30am
- Open by arrangement (01575 500267)

23 KINGOLDRUM PARISH CHURCH

Kingoldrum
DD8 5HW

NO 334 550

Church of Scotland

Linked with Airlie (2), Glenisla (18), Kilry (22), Lintrathen (29), Ruthven (41)

On B951 in centre of village

There has been a church in Kingoldrum since earliest times. A carved stone coffin lid found in the churchyard dates to the 12th or 13th century. The present church of 1840 is a small, oblong, Gothic church with a pinnacled belfry and projecting porches. Pews and panelling were the gift of Betty Sherriff, in memory of her husband, and the pulpit fall in memory of her parents.

- Sunday: 6.30pm in rotation with Airlie, Glenisla, Lintrathen and Ruthven
- Open by arrangement (01575 560260)

24 KIRRIEMUIR OLD PARISH CHURCH

Bank Street
Kirriemuir
DD8 4BG

NO 386 539

Church of Scotland

www.gkopc.co.uk

Linked with Cortachy (11), Glen Prosen (19), Memus (32)

Behind Bank Street's shops

Ninth-century stones were found when the church was rebuilt on this earlier Christian site in 1788 to a design by James Playfair, father of William Henry Playfair. The steeple was completed in 1790. Stained glass includes windows by William Wilson. Interesting kirkyard, the earliest stone dating from 1613.

- Sunday: 9.00am and 11.15am
- Open Monday to Friday 10.00am–12.00 noon, and Tuesday to Thursday 2.00–4.00pm (call at office if door locked) (01575 572819)

25 ST MARY'S CHURCH, KIRRIEMUIR

West Hillbank
Kirriemuir
DD8 4HX

NO 383 544

Scottish Episcopal

Linked with St John's, Forfar (14), St Margaret's, Lunanhead (30)

Finely detailed Gothic Revival church by Sir Ninian Comper, 1903, built to replace classical church of 1797 destroyed by fire. High-quality furnishings including stained glass by Comper and William Wilson. 2-manual tracker organ, Hamilton of Edinburgh, 1906. Sanctus bell, 1741. Conspicuous red sandstone bell-tower.

- Sunday: 10.00am on 1st, 2nd and 3rd Sunday of the month; 10.00am and 11.30am on 4th and 5th Sunday; Wednesday: 10.00am
- Key at Rectory, 128 Glengate, or 91 Glengate, Kirriemuir (01575 540255)

26 ST ANDREW'S CHURCH, KIRRIEMUIR

Glamis Road
Kirriemuir
DD8 5BN

NO 386 535

Church of Scotland

www.standrews-kirriemuir.org.uk

Linked with Tannadice (43)

Late Gothic-style church (originally the South United Free Church) with an 18-metre (60-ft) tower by Patrick Thoms, 1903. It replaced an earlier church (the South Free Church) built in 1843 for those who left the South Church (across the road) at the 'Disruption'. In the grounds are the headstones of Rev. Daniel Cormick, first minister of the South Free Church, and of Rev. A. Duff, minister of the South Church.

- Sunday: 11.15am
- Open daily 9.00am–5.00pm (01575 572961)

C   

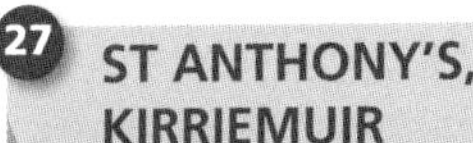

27 ST ANTHONY'S, KIRRIEMUIR

St Mary's Close
Kirriemuir
DD8 4GW

NO 383 543

Roman Catholic

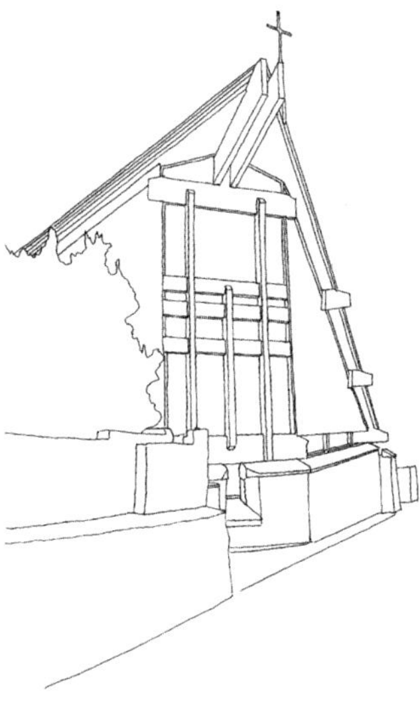

Linked with St Fergus's, Forfar (15)

Rectangular red sandstone church by local architect James F. Stephen, opened 1987, replacing earlier wooden church. Dedicated to St Anthony of Padua. Semi-circular seating and red granite altar. Stained glass, Stations of the Cross and statue of St Anthony by local artists.

- Sunday: 9.30am
- Open during daylight hours (01307 462104)

28 LIFF CHURCH

Church Road
Liff
DD2 5NN

NO 333 328

Church of Scotland

Linked with St Marnock's, Fowlis Easter (16), Lundie (31), Muirhead (38)

South end of village

Built 1839 to a design by William MacKenzie of Perth, to replace an earlier structure. The style is English Gothic with a 33-metre (108-ft) stone spire. Inside is a horseshoe gallery. Four stained-glass windows by J. & W. Guthrie of Glasgow. Organ 1880 by Alexander Young. Old priest's house, now a ruin, in neighbouring garden.

- Sunday: 10.00am in March, April, June, July and October
- Open by arrangement (01382 580210)

29 LINTRATHEN PARISH CHURCH

Lintrathen
DD8 5JH

NO 286 546

Church of Scotland

Linked with Airlie (2), Glenisla (18), Kilry (22), Kingoldrum (23), Ruthven (41)

Bridgend of Lintrathen

Beautiful wooded setting near the banks of Lintrathen Loch. Small, oblong, Gothic church of 1802, remodelled and extended to T-plan in 1875.

- Sunday: 6.30pm in rotation with Airlie, Glenisla, Kingoldrum and Ruthven
- Open by arrangement (01575 500267)

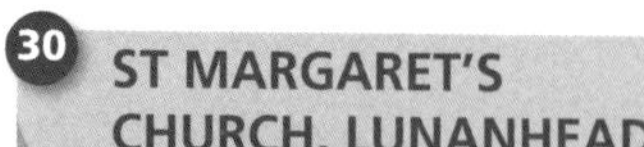

30 ST MARGARET'S CHURCH, LUNANHEAD

Carsebarracks
Lunanhead
DD8 3NU

NO 476 522

Scottish Episcopal

Linked with St John's, Forfar (14), St Mary's, Kirriemuir (25)

On B9134, 1.6km (1 mile) east of Forfar

Built in the planned village of Carsebarracks on the site of an earlier chapel in 1907 by the builder/architect William L. McLean of Forfar. Stained-glass window of the Crucifixion by A. D. Fleming of London, 1913. Mural by Miss W. M. Watson of Edinburgh, 1909.

- Sunday: 2.00pm on 1st and 3rd Sunday of the month, excluding July and August
- Open by arrangement (01307 463440)

31 LUNDIE CHURCH

St Laurence

Lundie
DD2 5NW

NO 291 366

Church of Scotland

Linked with St Marnock's, Fowlis Easter (16), Liff (28), Muirhead (38)

1.6km (1 mile) north of A923

Belonging to the Priory of St Andrews, the medieval church was dedicated to St Laurence. It was restored in 1892, when the porch and bellcote were added. Framed texts from the Psalms and Lord's Prayer, 1892. A stained-glass window depicting St John looks south, with a war memorial on the north wall. The reformer, Paul Methven, administered the Sacrament in 1558.

- Sunday: 9.00am
- Open by arrangement (01382 580210)

32 MEMUS CHURCH

Memus
DD8 3TY

NO 427 590

Church of Scotland

www.gkopc.co.uk

Linked with Cortachy (11), Glen Prosen (19), Kirriemuir Old (24)

In centre of village

Memus Church was built as the Free Church of Tannadice in 1843 in an outlying part of the parish. It is a plain rectangular building free of external ornamentation apart from the bellcote. The internal furnishings are of very fine pitch-pine. The church had only two ministers in 103 years.

- Sunday: 10.30am on 1st and 3rd Sunday of the month
- Open by arrangement (01575 572819)

33 HOLY TRINITY CHURCH, MONIFIETH

High Street
Monifieth
DD5 4AB

NO 499 327

Scottish Episcopal

www.holytrinitymonifieth.org

Black and white half-timbered-style building by Mills & Shepherd, 1909. Originally intended as church hall, adapted to church. Pleasant sheltered garden.

- Sunday: 8.00am and 10.30am
- Open daily (01382 533217)

34 ST BRIDE'S CHURCH, MONIFIETH

6–8 Brook Street
Monifieth
DD5 4BD

NO 499 325

Roman Catholic

The original church was established in 1880 in a converted cottage, which became the hall when the new church was built. A light airy building, 1983, it was designed by Brocks Bros of Leeds. Stained glass by Gail Donovan.

- Saturday: 9.30am and 6.00pm; Sunday: 10.30am and 6.15pm; Monday to Friday: 10.00am
- Open daily 8.30am–7.30pm (01241 873013)

MONTROSE OLD AND ST ANDREW'S CHURCH

Montrose Old

High Street
Montrose
DD10 8LJ

NO 715 578

Church of Scotland

www.oldandstandrews.com

Built 1793 by John Gibson with a 'lovely flying-buttressed spire (J. Gillespie Graham, 1832) which is Montrose's town-mark' (Colin McWilliam, *Scottish Townscape*).

- Sunday: 11.00am, also 6.30pm on last Sunday of the month
- Open June to August, Monday to Friday 2.00–4.30pm

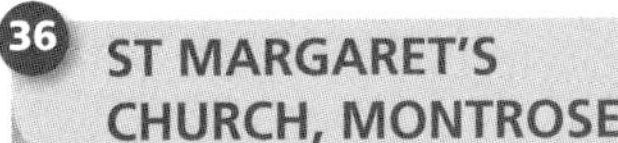

36 ST MARGARET'S CHURCH, MONTROSE

23 Market Street
Montrose
DD10 8NB

NO 716 581

Roman Catholic

Linked with St Ninian's, Brechin (10)

Opened 1886; architect Robert Keith. Font by David Lamb. Painting of St Margaret for 900th anniversary in 1993.

- Sunday: 11.30am; Monday, Friday and Saturday: 10.00am
- Open 7.30am–6.00pm; entry restricted to back of church (01674 672208)

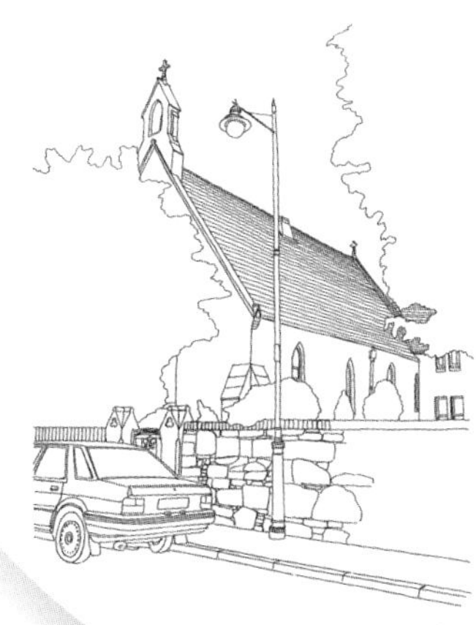

KNOX UNITED FREE CHURCH, MONTROSE

Mill Street
Montrose
DD10 8NE

NO 716 582

United Free Church

Linked with Ferryden UFC (12)

Junction with John Street

In simple Perpendicular Gothic style with pinnacle and three gables on the street façade. Opened 1851 as Mill Street United Presbyterian Church; became St Luke's United Free Church in 1900; closed 1953 and reopened as Knox United Free Church in 1954. Stained glass depicting the Gospel stories of St Luke. Carved wooden pulpit and reredos.

- Sunday: 11.00am
- Open by arrangement (01674 673772)

MUIRHEAD CHURCH

149 Coupar Angus Road
Muirhead of Liff
DD2 5QN

NO 342 344

Church of Scotland

Linked with St Marnock's, Fowlis Easter (16), Liff (28), Lundie (31)

South side of A923

After the Disruption in 1843, the church was built with stones given and transported by local farmers. In 1960, it was reconditioned, and in 1997 the vestry and choir-room were converted into a hall, and a new vestry and toilets added.

- Sunday: 11.30am
- Open by arrangement (01382 580210)

39 MURROES & TEALING PARISH CHURCH

Murroes
DD5 3PB

NO 461 351

Church of Scotland

www.sidlawchurches.com/pages/worship/1.php

Linked with Auchterhouse (7)

On B978, north of Broughty Ferry

T-plan church by William Smith, 1848, on a site occupied by a church for 750 years. Church records from 1202. Interesting gravestones and coping on churchyard wall carved with texts in English, Latin and Greek. Interior has pews with doors, impressive stained-glass windows and small pipe organ in gallery. Former coach-house and stables restored to provide hall, chapel, kitchen and toilet facilities.

- Sunday: 9.30am on 1st and 3rd Sunday of the month, 11.00am on 2nd and 4th Sunday
- Open by arrangement (01382 456838)

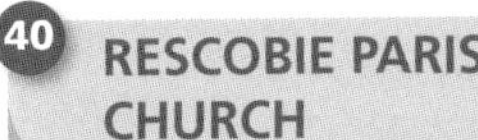

40 RESCOBIE PARISH CHURCH

Rescobie
DD8 2TD

NO 509 521

Church of Scotland

Linked with Aberlemno (1), Guthrie (20)

5km (3 miles) east of Forfar on B9113

Built 1820 to a Telford design, incorporating a 17th-century mural monument in the south wall. Very fine oak ceiling. Single-manual pipe organ by Millar of Dundee.

- Sunday: 10.00am or 11.30am (times change monthly; please contact minister for details)
- Open by arrangement (01241 828243)

41 RUTHVEN CHURCH

Ruthven
PH12 8RQ

NO 286 489

Church of Scotland

Linked with Airlie (2), Glenisla (18), Kilry (22), Kingoldrum (23), Lintrathen (29)

On A926 between Rattray and Kirriemuir

Ruthven parish was first noted in 1180. The present red sandstone church of 1859 is the fourth on this site overlooking the River Isla. Two ancient stone crosses in the west wall, and headstones in the graveyard dating from the early 17th century. Annual music festival mid-June weekend.

- Sunday: 6.30pm in rotation with Airlie, Glenisla, Kingoldrum and Lintrathen
- Open by arrangement (01828 632558)

42 STRACATHRO PARISH CHURCH

Stracathro
DD9 7QE

NO 618 658

Church of Scotland

www.brechincathedral.org.uk/

Linked with Brechin Cathedral (9)

1.6km (1 mile) north-west of Stracathro Hospital; 1.6km (1 mile) east of Inchbare

Built within the site of a Roman fort (c. AD 80–230). The current building is rectangular in red sandstone with a bellcote on the west gable. The bell was 'made for the Kirk of Stracathro on 1st May 1793 by T. Mears of London'. The church was opened in 1799 and extended in 1878. Internal alterations, 1970, with furniture from St Andrew's Church of Scotland in Fairlie, Ayrshire.

- Sunday: 9.30am on 2nd Sunday of the month
- Open by arrangement (01356 629360) (Monday to Friday 10.00am–12.00 noon)

TANNADICE CHURCH

Oathlaw Tannadice Church

Southesk Road
Tannadice
DD8 3TA

NO 475 581

Church of Scotland

www.standrews-kirriemuir.org.uk

Linked with St Andrew's, Kirriemuir (26)

11km (7 miles) north of Forfar on B957

A place of Christian worship since the 7th century. A monastery was recorded in 1187, and the Kirk of Tanatheys was consecrated in 1242. Present church by John Carver built 1866, extended 2003. St Columba and St Francis windows, 1976, in memory of 2nd Lord Forres of Glenogil. War memorial windows on north wall by James Ballantine, 1923, and Neil Hamilton, 1949. Since 2008, the church has hosted a post office in the vestibule on Monday, 3.00–5.00pm.

- Sunday: 9.45am
- Open by arrangement (01307 850345)

ST MARY'S CHURCH, BROUGHTY FERRY

164 Queen Street
Broughty Ferry
DD5 1AJ

NO 461 310

Scottish Episcopal

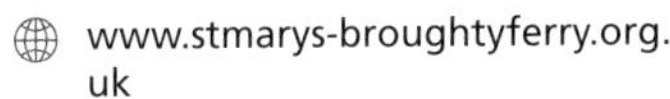

www.stmarys-broughtyferry.org.uk

A930

Pretty Episcopal church of nave and chancel, designed by Sir George Gilbert Scott, 1858, and enlarged 1870. Sir Robert Lorimer extended the chancel, 1911. The pulpit, screen, choir stalls and reredos are all by Lorimer. Garden of Remembrance. Good collection of Victorian and modern stained glass.

- Sunday: 8.30am, 11.00am and 6.00pm; Wednesday and Thursday: 10.00am
- Open 9.00am–5.00pm most days, or by arrangement (01382 778674)

45 OUR LADY OF GOOD COUNSEL, BROUGHTY FERRY

Westfield Road
Broughty Ferry
DD5 1ED

NO 458 309

Roman Catholic

Designed by T. M. Cappon in a Gothic style, 1904. The tower at the west end has a statue of the Madonna and Child.

- Sunday: 9.00am and 11.00am; Monday, Wednesday, Friday: 9.00am; Tuesday, Thursday, Saturday: 10.00am
- Open by arrangement (01382 778750)

46 DUNDEE PARISH CHURCH

St Mary's

Nethergate
Dundee
DD1 4DG

NO 401 301

Church of Scotland

www.dundeestmarys.co.uk

North of Discovery Point and railway station

Founded in 1190 by the Earl of Huntingdon. Rebuilt in 1844 by William Burn in an accomplished Gothic style. Beautiful 19th- and 20th-century stained glass, including windows by Burne-Jones, Cottier, Powell & Sons and T. S. Halliday. War memorial, 1914–18. Impressive organ installed 1865. Reading desk with interesting history.

- Sunday: 10.30am
- Open June to August, Wednesday and Saturday 2.00–5.00pm (01382 226271)

ST PAUL'S CATHEDRAL, DUNDEE

Castlehill, 1 High Street
Dundee
DD1 1TD

NO 404 303

Scottish Episcopal

www.stpaulscathedraldundee.org

East end of High Street at junction with Commercial Street

Designed by Sir George Gilbert Scott in 1853, the cathedral stands on the site of Dundee's ancient castle. Gothic in style, but Gothic with a difference: tall, graceful columns give an impression of lightness and airiness. Splendid reredos mosaic by Salviati of Venice. Stained glass including windows by Hardman and Scott & Draper. Organ by Hill, 1865, rebuilt by Hill, Norman & Beard, 1976.

- Sunday: 11.00am and 6.30pm; Tuesday to Friday: 1.10pm
- Open Tuesday to Saturday 11.00am–3.00pm (01382 224486)

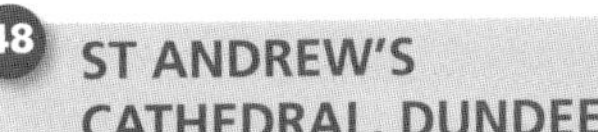

48 ST ANDREW'S CATHEDRAL, DUNDEE

150 Nethergate
Dundee
DD1 4EA

NO 400 299

Roman Catholic

Designed by George Mathewson in 1835; the façade is in Perpendicular Gothic style with buttresses and pinnacles. Impressive arcaded interior, with seating for 1,200. Outstanding 19th- and 20th-century stained glass by Mayer of Munich.

- Sunday: 11.30am and 7.00pm; weekdays: 10.00am
- Open Monday to Saturday 9.00am–3.00pm (01382 225228)

BALGAY PARISH CHURCH, DUNDEE

St Thomas's

Tullideph Road
Dundee
DD2 2PP

NO 380 314

Church of Scotland

www.balgaychurch.org.uk/

Junction with Lochee Road

Originally built as St Thomas's Church, Balgay Parish Church was opened for worship on 29 December 1902. Cruciform, designed by local architects Johnston & Baxter. Stained-glass windows designed by Susan Bradbury were installed in 1995 and 2007. 3-manual Makin digital organ installed, 1999.

- Sunday: 11.00am
- Open by arrangement (01382 668806)

MEADOWSIDE ST PAUL'S, DUNDEE

114–116 Nethergate
Dundee
DD1 4EH

NO 401 300

Church of Scotland

www.mspdundee.com

Built in 1852, replacing the Mariners' Church, to a design by Charles Wilson. The fine spire terminates the elevation of Nethergate. Organ by Walker & Co., 1902, overhauled by Rushworth & Dreaper, 1971. Stained glass, some by Jones & Willis, and by Alexander Russell. Sets of tapestried pulpit falls, tapestry kneelers. Doorway mosaics by Elizabeth McFall.

- Sunday: 11.00am
- Open Wednesday 12.00 noon–1.30pm for prayer and meditation, or by arrangement (01382 825848)

 (by arrangement)

ST ANDREW'S PARISH CHURCH, DUNDEE

2 King Street
Dundee
DD1 2JB

NO 404 307

Church of Scotland

www.standrewschurch.co.uk

Next to Wellgate Shopping Centre

Trades' kirk with interesting history, dating from 1774; built by Samuel Bell with plans by James Craig, Edinburgh. Beautiful stained glass. Includes former Glasite Kirk of 1777 (the Kail Kirk), now part of the church-hall complex. Handsome spire with peal of fine musical bells. Lovely gardens.

- Sunday: 11.00am all year; also 9.30am June, July and August
- Open Tuesday, Thursday and Saturday 10.00am–12.00 noon all year (01382 641695)

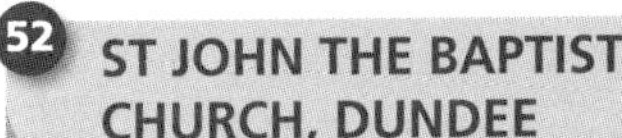

ST JOHN THE BAPTIST CHURCH, DUNDEE

116 Albert Street
Dundee
DD4 6QN

NO 411 314

Scottish Episcopal

A929, just north of city centre

The present building was consecrated in 1886. Designed with a French-style roof by Rev. Edward Sugden, 1885. The sanctuary and chancel are panelled in late Gothic style, the details suggested by the woodwork in King's College Chapel, Aberdeen. Reredos by William Hole. The font cover is a splendid carved wooden spire.

- Sunday: 10.15am; Thursday: 10.00am
- Open Thursday 9.00–11.00am, other times by arrangement (01382 455656)

53 ST MARGARET'S, LOCHEE, DUNDEE

**17/19 Ancrum Road, Lochee
Dundee
DD2 2JL**

NO 382 312

Scottish Episcopal

A923, north-west of city centre

Nave-and-chancel church, designed by Rev. E. Sugden, 1888, in Gothic Revival style. Wooden 18th-century Flemish pulpit. The font, in the form of an angel holding a large shell, is a copy of a font by Danish artist Bertel Thorvaldsen in Copenhagen Cathedral. Organ by Wood Wordsworth of Leeds, built 1890 and installed 1979.

- Sunday: 11.00am; Tuesday: 10.00am; Thursday: 10.00am
- Open by arrangement (01382 667227)

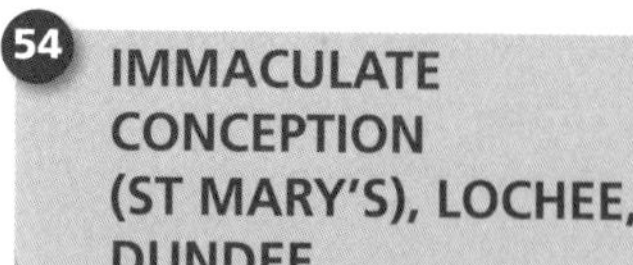

54 IMMACULATE CONCEPTION (ST MARY'S), LOCHEE, DUNDEE

**41 High Street, Lochee
Dundee
DD2 3AP**

NO 380 314

Roman Catholic

A923, north-west of city centre

Remarkable Gothic Revival church of 1866 by Joseph A. Hansom, ennobled by a polygonal chancel which soars up into the spire and gives a contrast between the dark nave and well-lit chancel. Flamboyant altarpiece by A. B. Wall of Cheltenham, 1897. Stained glass by Mayer of Munich. Floodlit well 12 metres deep.

- Saturday: 6.00pm; Sunday: 11.30am; Monday to Saturday: 10.00am
- Open by arrangement (01382 611282)

ST MARY MAGDALENE, DUNDEE

Constitution Road
Dundee
DD1 5RR

NO 399 306

Scottish Episcopal

http://stmmdundee.org.uk

Junction with Dudhope Crescent Road

Built 1867 by local architects Edward & Robertson for the Catholic Apostolic Church; it has been Scottish Episcopal since 1952. Very fine organ, originally by Conacher, rebuilt in 1937 by Rothwell and again in 1989 by Nicholson. Beautiful stained glass; 27 windows of demolished churches installed 1985–2000 from the Stained Glass Museum in Ely and the Church of Wales.

- Sunday: 8.00am, 11.00am and 6.30pm; Wednesday: 10.00am
- Open Monday to Friday 5.00–9.00pm, Saturday 10.00am–1.00pm; enter via garden gate (01382 223510)

ST PETER'S FREE CHURCH, DUNDEE

St Peter Street
Dundee
DD1 4JJ

NO 390 298

Free Church of Scotland

www.stpeters-dundee.org.uk

Off Perth Road, 1.6km (1 mile) west of city centre

Built by Hean Brothers, 1836, this was the seat of Rev. Robert McCheyne (1813–43), a major player in the Evangelical revival, who made these sober rafters ring. Elegant, classical church with a gallery carried on cast-iron columns. Original pulpit. The plain simplicity of the building is ennobled by the tower and stone spire against its east gable.

- Sunday: 11.00am and 6.30pm; Wednesday: 7.30pm
- Open Monday 1.30–4.00pm and Tuesday to Thursday 9.30am–3.30pm (01382 861401)

ST SALVADOR'S CHURCH, DUNDEE

**St Salvador's Street
Dundee
DD3 7EW**

NO 403 313

Scottish Episcopal

www.stsalvadors.com

Entrance off Carnegie Street

Church in early Arts & Crafts Gothic by G. F. Bodley, 1868. Glorious painted interior with stencilled decoration to the walls and ceiling, the splendour and richness increasing in the chancel and apse. Organ by Wadsworth & Maskell, 1882, recently restored.

- Sunday: 9.00am and 11.00am; Tuesday: 7.00pm; Wednesday: 10.00am
- Open Saturday mornings (01382 221785)

THE STEEPLE CHURCH, DUNDEE

**Nethergate
Dundee
DD1 4DG**

NO 402 301

Church of Scotland

www.thesteeplechurch.org.uk

A landmark, known as 'Old Steeple'. The church building dates from 1788, by Samuel Bell. The bright, colourful appearance of the sanctuary and the Welcoming Hall derives from the renovations carried out at the time of the congregation's bicentenary in 1989. Entry through 15th-century St Mary's Tower.

- Sunday: 11.00am and 7.00pm
- Open July to August, Tuesday and Saturday 12.00 noon–3.00pm (01382 778240)

St John's Kirk of Perth 108

Brechin Cathedral 9

Aberfeldy Parish Church 61

St Leonard's-in-the-Fields, Perth 113

Collace Parish Church 78

St Ninian's Cathedral, Perth 109

Dunkeld Cathedral 86

Tannadice Church 43

Weem Church 128

Pitlochry Baptist Church 119

Amulree Kirk 66

St Michael & All Angels, Ballintuim 70

Aberlemno Parish Church 1

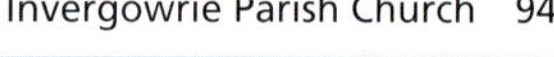

Invergowrie Parish Church 94

Pitlochry Church 117

St Salvador's Church, Dundee 57

Holy Trinity, Pitlochry 118

Kettins Parish Church 96

Kinnoull Parish Church 111

59 STOBSWELL PARISH CHURCH, DUNDEE

172 Albert Street
Dundee
DD4 6QW

NO 411 315

Church of Scotland

www.stobswellchurch.org.uk

Junction of Dura Street and Forfar Road

Originally Ogilvie Free Church, on a prominent island site, by Charles E. and Thomas S. Robertson, 1874. Characterful, stone-built L-shaped church with a spire. Extensive refurbishment has now created within the main church building four halls, a fully equipped office and a kitchen, in addition to the sanctuary and vestry. Fine stained-glass windows by William Wilson.

- Sunday: 11.00am (July and August 10.30am)
- Open by arrangement (01382 308630)

60 ABERDALGIE CHURCH

Aberdalgie
PH2 0QD

NO 079 203

Church of Scotland

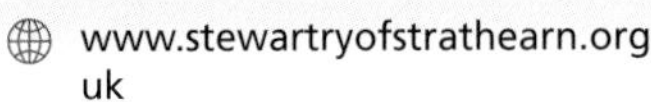

www.stewartryofstrathearn.org.uk

Linked with Aberuthven (63), Dunning (87), Forteviot (88)

Off B9112

Nestling in the Earn Valley on a site of enduring worship for centuries, the present church was built by the Earl of Kinnoull in 1773. A T-plan church of local sandstone features a fine laird's loft and Georgian retiring room. 14th-century Tournai marble Oliphant monument. Sir Robert Lorimer remodelled the interior in 1929. Extensive use of Austrian oak gives the church a sense of peace and simple dignity. Renovations, 1994.

- Sunday: 11.15am
- Open Tuesday and Thursday 9.00am–1.00pm or by arrangement (01738 621674)

61 ABERFELDY PARISH CHURCH

**Taybridge Road
Aberfeldy
PH15 2BH**

NN 854 491

Church of Scotland

Linked with Amulree (66), Weem (128)

Built in 1843 as a Free church; the galleries were removed, the floor area reduced and the roof lowered when it was made a church hall after a union of congregations in the 1960s. Major alterations in 2005 gave the sanctuary its previous floor area, and welcome area, crèche, halls and catering facilities in a new extension.

- Sunday: 11.15am and 6.30pm
- Open 9.00am–12.30pm Monday to Thursday, or by arrangement (01887 820656)

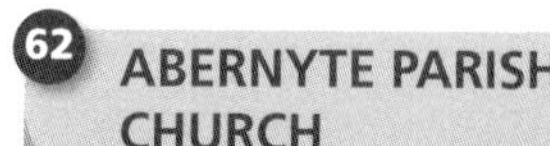

62 ABERNYTE PARISH CHURCH

Carse Parish

**Abernyte
PH14 9SS**

NO 267 311

Church of Scotland

www.carsechurches.com

Linked with Inchture (93), Kinnaird (99)

800 metres (½ mile) east of village

The present church was built in 1736 to replace a building of pre-1400, although there may have been a Celtic church here much earlier. The present cruciform shape was established in 1837 when the chancel was added and the church reorientated. Stained glass, including a window of 2007 of the Abernyte countryside. Wall hangings of the 1990s.

- Sunday: 11.00am
- Open daily (01828 686509)

63 ABERUTHVEN CHURCH

Aberuthven
PH3 1HH

NN 979 155

Church of Scotland

www.stewartryofstrathearn.org.uk

Linked with Aberdalgie (60), Dunning (87), Forteviot (88)

3km (2 miles) from Auchterarder on A824

The present modest church was built in 1991. The remains of the medieval parish church of St Kattan are to the west of the village with the beautifully detailed classical Montrose Mausoleum of the 1730s by William Adam.

- Sunday: 12.00 noon
- Open by arrangement (01738 621674)

64 ALYTH PARISH CHURCH

Kirk Brae
Alyth
PH11 8DS

NO 243 488

Church of Scotland

www.alythparishchurch.org.uk

In a prominent position overlooking the town, and completed in 1839 to a design by Thomas Hamilton. Gothic, with Romanesque influences and an unusually high spire. 8th- or 9th-century Pictish stone stands 1.2 metres (4ft) high in the vestibule. 3-manual organ by Harrison & Harrison, 1890. Family-history resource centre.

- Sunday: 11.00am; also 6.00pm on 1st Sunday of the month (except June, July and August)
- Open July and August, Saturday 10.00am–12.00 noon, Sunday 2.00–4.00pm (01828 632104)

65 ST NINIAN'S, ALYTH

St Ninian's Road
Alyth
PH11 8AP

NO 247 483

Scottish Episcopal

www.abcsaints.org.uk

Linked with St Michael's, Ballintuim (70), St Catharine's, Blairgowrie (73), St Anne's, Coupar Angus (80)

Off Main Street

Neo-Norman church by David Bryce, 1857, with nave and chancel with apse. The stone font of 1863 was moved here from St Margaret's, Meigle. Three windows in the chancel are by O'Connor, c. 1860; the wheel window in the west gable is by Clayton & Bell. Organ, John R. Miller, 1909. Marble and brass memorials.

- Sunday: 11.00am; Thursday: 11.00am
- Open Sunday 12.30–5.30pm, May to October (01250 874583)

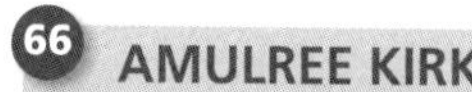

66 AMULREE KIRK

Amulree
PH8 0BZ

NN 899 366

Church of Scotland

Linked with Aberfeldy (61), Weem (128)

On A822 Crieff–Dunkeld road

Built in 1743. The scantily populated setting reminds us of the large numbers who emigrated to Canada, as commemorated in copies of old records available for inspection in the church. The beams from the Black Wood of Rannoch were first used in the construction of Wade's bridge over the Tay in Aberfeldy. Attractive stained-glass window of Faith, Hope and Love.

- Sunday: 2.15pm fortnightly
- Open daily (01887 820656)

67 ARDOCH PARISH CHURCH

Feddal Road
Braco
PH2 0QD

NN 837 098

Church of Scotland

B8033 Braco–Kinbuck road

Officially opened for worship in 1781 as a chapel of ease, the church was originally a rectangular building. The bellcote was added in 1836 and a chancel built on the east end by William Simpson of Stirling in 1890. The most recent addition is the church hall, built 1985.

- Sunday: 11.30am in even-numbered years, 10.00am in odd-numbered years
- Open by arrangement (01786 880349)

68 ST KESSOG'S CHURCH, AUCHTERARDER

High Street
Auchterarder
PH3 1AD

NN 942 128

Scottish Episcopal

www.stkessogs.co.uk

Linked with St James's, Muthill (107)

50 metres off High Street

Neat Gothic church, built 1897, architect Alexander Ross of Inverness. The cream window and door margins contrast with the dark stone of the walls. Beautiful altar and reredos of Caen stone by Alexander Neilson, both richly decorated with Florentine mosaic. Rood screen of white stone. East and west windows by Kempe of London. In quiet grounds and garden.

- Sunday: January to June 9.30am, July to December 11.00am
- Open July and August, Monday to Friday 2.00–4.00pm, or by arrangement (01764 662525)

69 AUCHTERGAVEN & MONEYDIE PARISH CHURCH

Bankfoot Church Centre

Tulliebelton Road
Bankfoot
PH1 4BS

NO 062 349

Church of Scotland

www.bankfootchurch.org.uk/

On western edge of village

New eco-friendly church, opened in October 2008, following destruction by fire of original church in 2004. Designed by Raymond Angus, the building incorporates cutting-edge technology and many ecological features, including a ground-source heat pump, two wind turbines and rainwater harvesting. Many furnishings created from a donated oak tree.

- Sunday: 10.30am
- Open Monday to Friday 9.30am–1.30pm (01738 788017)

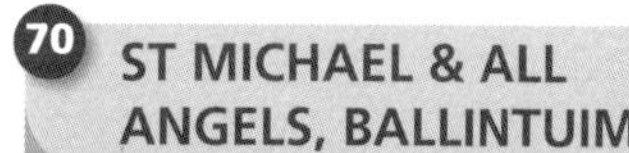

70 ST MICHAEL & ALL ANGELS, BALLINTUIM

Ballintuim
PH10 7NN

NO 101 552

Scottish Episcopal

www.abcsaints.org.uk

Linked with St Ninian's, Alyth (65), St Catharine's, Blairgowrie (73), St Anne's, Coupar Angus (80)

On A924, 6.5km (4 miles) north of Bridge of Cally

Beautiful church set in rural Perthshire. Foundation stone laid September 1898; completed using stone from three local derelict crofts; total cost less than £500. Simple wooden interior with ornate candlesticks either side of the altar.

- Sunday: 10.30am May to October
- Open by arrangement (01250 874583)

71 ST MARY'S CHURCH, BIRNAM

Perth Road
Birnam
PH8 0BJ

NO 032 418

Scottish Episcopal

http://stmarysbirnam.org.uk/

Linked with St Andrew's, Strathtay (125)

In centre of village

Main church and clock-tower to a design by William Slater, 1858, with north aisle by Norman & Beddoe, 1883. Slater font and cover, Kempe east window, William Morris windows to Burne-Jones designs. Organ originally by Forster & Andrews, 1874. Three-bell chime, clock by James Ramsay of Dundee, 1882. Beautifully kept churchyard.

- Sunday: 9.45am; Wednesday: 9.30am
- Open by arrangement (01738 710726)

72 BLAIRGOWRIE PARISH CHURCH

James Street
Blairgowrie
PH10 6EZ

NO 177 454

Church of Scotland

www.blairgowrieparish.org.uk

The present building, designed by D. & J. R. MacMillan, was completed in 1904 in Early English Gothic style with tower and spire, transepts, aisles, apse and a small gallery. Five stained-glass windows in the apse depict scenes from the life of Moses. Norman & Beard organ, 1907, rebuilt 1989 by A. F. Edmonstone. The first Free Church of Blairgowrie is now the hall.

- Sunday: 11.00am
- Open by arrangement (01250 872729)

73 ST CATHARINE'S, BLAIRGOWRIE

George Street
Blairgowrie
PH10 6HA

NO 177 454

Scottish Episcopal

www.abcsaints.org.uk

Linked with St Ninian's, Alyth (65), St Michael's, Ballintuim (70), St Anne's, Coupar Angus (80)

On corner of Brown Street

Built in 1842–3 by the incumbent, Rev. John Marshall, and designed by his 14-year-old stepson, John Henderson. The Gothic-style church has a nave and a chancel. The east window is possibly by John Warrington (1796–1869). On the west wall is panelling of the 15th or 16th century, probably Italian, depicting the Ascension. It was placed here in 1894.

- Sunday: 9.30am, except 5th Sunday of the month (see website for venue); Wednesday: 11.30am, daily prayer 9.00am
- Open all day, every day, except after Sunday service (01250 874583)

  (in Community Centre) 

 BRAES OF RANNOCH PARISH CHURCH

Bridge of Gaur
PH17 2QB

NN 507 566

Church of Scotland

Linked with Foss (89), Old Church of Rannoch (122)

South Loch Road at head of loch

Built in 1907, architect Peter Macgregor Chalmers, the church has a special atmosphere of peace and beauty. The bellcote is from an earlier building of 1776. Rothwell pipe organ from Urquhart Church, Elgin, rebuilt 1991 by David Loosley. This was the only charge of Rev. Archibald Eneas Robertson (1907–20), first official ascender of all 'Munros' in Scotland (nowadays 283 peaks over 914 metres, 3,000 ft).

- Sunday: 9.45am
- Open daily (01882 632381)

75 CAPUTH PARISH CHURCH

Caputh
PH1 4JH

NO 088 401

Church of Scotland

Linked with Kinclaven (98)

6.5km (4 miles) east of Dunkeld on A984

There has been a church in Caputh since the 9th century. The present building was started in 1798, the aisle and tower added in 1865 and the windows altered in 1918. The interior, by Heiton, 1913, has oak furnishings and stained-glass windows. Organ by James Bruce of Edinburgh, c. 1830.

- Sunday: 11.15am
- Open by arrangement

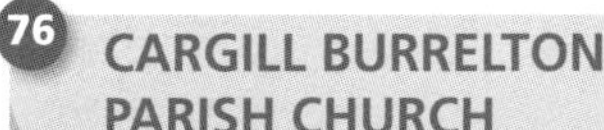

76 CARGILL BURRELTON PARISH CHURCH

Station Road
Woodside
PH13 9NQ

NO 202 377

Church of Scotland

www.cbcollace.co.uk

Linked with Collace (78)

Off A94 Perth to Coupar Angus road

In a picturesque setting, this rectangular church has Gothic windows and an octagonal belfry. Originally built as Burrelton Free Church in 1854–5; Church of Scotland since 1929, it united with Cargill in 1980. Two stained-glass windows by William Meigle & Son. Allen organ. Embroidered pulpit falls by church member Ishbel Chambers.

- Sunday: 10.00am
- Open by arrangement (01828 627773)

77 CLEISH CHURCH

Cleish
KY13 0LR

NT 095 981

Church of Scotland

http://cleishchurch.com/

Off B9097, 3km (2 miles) west from Junction 5 of M90

Built on 13th-century site in 1832, designed by D. McIntosh. Handsome hall-church with Perpendicular Gothic detail. Square tower by Hardy & Wight added in 1897. Organ and lights from St Giles', Edinburgh. The hymn 'Jesus, tender Shepherd, hear me' was written by former minister's wife, Mary Lundie Duncan, in the manse.

- Sunday: 11.15am
- Open daily 10.00am–5.00pm (01577 850231)

   (in halls)  

78 COLLACE PARISH CHURCH

Kinrossie
PH2 6HU

NO 197 320

Church of Scotland

www.cbcollace.co.uk

Linked with Cargill Burrelton (76)

1.6km (1 mile) east of A94

Stone church with tower, built 1812–13 on site of an earlier church dedicated in 1242. Four-light stained-glass window of 1919 depicting scenes from the life of Christ. Remains of medieval building nearby with Norman archway, turned into the imposing mausoleum for the Nairne family in 1813. Important 17th- and 18th-century gravestones and small mort-house.

- Sunday: 11.15am
- Open by arrangement (01821 650236)

79 COMRIE PARISH CHURCH

Burrell Street
Comrie
PH6 2JP

NN 770 221

Church of Scotland

Linked with Dundurn (85)

Originally a Free church, designed and built 1879–81 by George T. Ewing on a site surrounded by attractive grounds overlooking the River Earn. Handsome church in dark masonry with pale dressed stone. The broad gable facing the street is complemented by a tall steeple. Organ by T. C. Lewis, built 1910 for the London Exhibition.

- Sunday: 10.00am
- Open daily (01764 679184)

ST ANNE'S, COUPAR ANGUS

Forfar Road
Coupar Angus
PH13 9AN

NO 224 403

Scottish Episcopal

www.abcsaints.org.uk

Linked with St Ninian's, Alyth (65), St Michael's, Ballintuim (70), St Catharine's, Blairgowrie (73)

A94 from Perth

Consecrated in 1848, St Anne's was designed by William Hay. In Gothic Revival style with a nave and chancel, it is similar to many Early English parish churches. Fine stained-glass windows by Alexander L. Russell, Clayton & Bell and Gordon Webster. Relief of the Last Supper in the reredos. Pipe organ by Harrison & Harrison, 1887.

- Sunday: 11.00am except 5th Sunday of the month (see website for venue)
- Open by arrangement (01250 874583)

81 CRIEFF PARISH CHURCH

Strathearn Terrace
Crieff
PH7 3BZ

NN 867 219

Church of Scotland

www.crieffparishchurch.org

The church's tall saddle-backed tower dominates the skyline of Crieff. Designed by local architect George T. Ewing and built, 1880–2, of Alloa stone. Organ, originally 1882 by Forster & Andrews, reconstructed 1964. Brilliant stained-glass windows, including some by Alfred Webster and Stephen Adam.

- Sunday: 9.30am, 11.00am and 6.30pm
- Open by arrangement (01764 653907)

 82 THE SEVENTH-DAY ADVENTIST CHURCH, CRIEFF

Gwydyr Road
Crieff
PH7 4BS

NN 861 224

Seventh-Day Adventist

www.crieffadventist.org.uk/

A beautiful modern church built in 1977 by Maranatha, an international group of retired people who travel the world building churches, schools and medical clinics. This building was constructed in 11 days; halfway through the week, the local bookmaker stopped taking bets on its completion date!

- Saturday: 11.15am
- Open by arrangement (01764 653257)

83 ST ANNE'S, DOWALLY

Dowally
PH9 0NT

NO 001 480

Church of Scotland

www.dunkeldcathedral.org.uk/dowally.htm

Linked with Dunkeld Cathedral (86), Little Dunkeld (101)

A9, 5km (3 miles) north of Dunkeld

Built in 1818 on the site of a 16th-century building, St Anne's is a small country church with a bright interior. The designer was probably John Stewart, although the church has been much altered since. The bell (still in use) and belfry came from the earlier church. Organ and chancel screens from Dunkeld Cathedral.

- Sunday: 2.00pm on 2nd, 4th and 5th Sunday of the month
- Open by arrangement (01796 482407)

84 DUNBARNEY PARISH CHURCH

Manse Road
Bridge of Earn
PH2 9DY

NO 130 185

Church of Scotland

Off main street

Prior to 1684, Dunbarney Parish Church stood a mile to the west in the burial ground. In 1684, a church was erected a few metres from the present building. The present rectangular plan church was built in 1787. Pedimented bellcote added, interior recast and other alterations, 1880. The pipe organ, built by John Miller, Dundee, was installed in 1929.

- Sunday: 9.30am
- Open by arrangement (01738 812223)

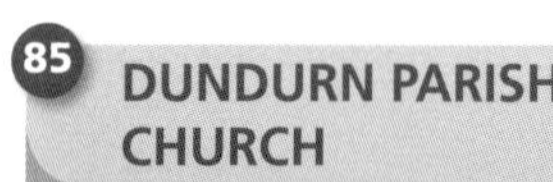

85 DUNDURN PARISH CHURCH

St Fillans
PH6 2NF

NN 697 241

Church of Scotland

Linked with Comrie (79)

East end of Loch Earn

Small, stone-built rectangular church with Gothic porch and belfry. Designed by G. T. Ewing and built in 1878. Of particular interest is the medieval stone font. Oak panelling, pulpit and communion table with Celtic knotwork. Set in grounds with striking view across Loch Earn.

- Sunday: 11.30am June to September, 12.00 noon October to May
- Open daily, Easter to October (01764 679184)

86 DUNKELD CATHEDRAL

Cathedral Street
Dunkeld
PH8 0AW

NO 024 426

Church of Scotland

www.dunkeldcathedral.org.uk

Linked with St Anne's, Dowally (83), Little Dunkeld (101)

The cathedral lies in a superb setting on the banks of the Tay. The restored choir, now used as the parish church, was completed in 1350. The chapter-house of 1469, adjacent to the choir, contains a small museum. The choir, completely renovated in 1907, contains a Lorimer screen and the tomb of the Wolf of Badenoch. The tower, ruined nave, south porch and grounds are in the care of Historic Scotland.

- Sunday: 11.00am Easter to Remembrance Sunday; also 6.30pm on 1st Sunday in June and September
- Open daily, summer 9.30am–7.00pm, winter 9.30am–4.00pm (01350 723222)

 (by arrangement)

87 DUNNING CHURCH

Perth Road
Dunning
PH2 0RY

NO 019 145

Church of Scotland

www.stewartryofstrathearn.org.uk

Linked with Aberdalgie (60), Aberuthven (63), Forteviot (88)

In centre of village

Built for the United Free Church in plain Gothic style, designed by William Laidlaw; foundation stone laid 1908. The church became Church of Scotland in 1929. Open timber roof and simple, well-crafted furnishings. Fine stained glass, including the west window of the Evangelists and a window to mark the end of the second Christian Millennium.

- Sunday: 10.30am
- Open by arrangement (01738 621674)

88 FORTEVIOT CHURCH

St Andrew's

Forteviot
PH2 9BT

NO 050 174

Church of Scotland

www.stewartryofstrathearn.org.uk

Linked with Aberdalgie (60), Aberuthven (63), Dunning (87)

On B935

In the 9th century, Kenneth MacAlpin had his palace here; and a basilica existed from the first half of the 8th century. This church, the third, was erected in 1778. It was remodelled in the mid-19th century. Celtic bell dated AD 900, one of five Scottish bronze bells. Medieval carved stones. The font is from the pre-Reformation church of Muckersie, which united with Forteviot in 1618. Organ by Hamilton of Edinburgh. Extensively renovated, 1994.

- Sunday: 10.00am
- Open by arrangement (01738 621674)

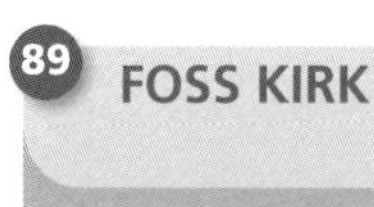

89 FOSS KIRK

Tummel Bridge
PH16 5NH

NN 790 581

Church of Scotland

Linked with Braes of Rannoch (74), Old Church of Rannoch (122)

Off B846, south of Tummel Bridge

Simple rectangular kirk with a bellcote on the west gable. A church on this site was founded AD 625 by St Chad and used until the Reformation. This fell into disrepair in 1580 and was rebuilt in 1824. Perth bell, 1824. Ancient graveyard behind the church with view of Loch Tummel.

- Sunday: 7.00pm on 1st and 3rd Sunday of the month, May to September; 2.30pm on 1st Sunday, October to April
- Open daily (01882 632381)

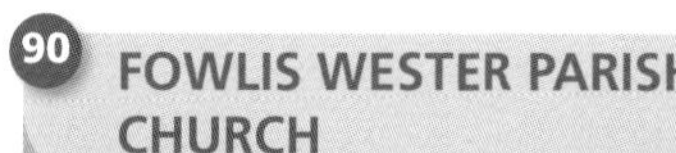

90 FOWLIS WESTER PARISH CHURCH

St Bean

Fowlis Wester
PH7 3NL

NN 928 241

Church of Scotland

Linked with Gask (91)

1.6km (1 mile) north of A85, 8km (5 miles) east of Crieff

St Bean (d. 720) was a grandson of the King of Leinster, Ireland, and preached among the Picts in this area. There has been a church on this site since those times. The church is a 13th-century building renovated in 1927 by Jeffrey Waddell of Glasgow with much Celtic ornament. It retains many of the original features, including a 'lepers' squint'. Pictish Cross under the north wall.

- Sunday: 11.30am
- Open by arrangement (01764 652116)

91 GASK PARISH CHURCH

Findo Gask Church

Findo Gask
PH7 3PH

NO 002 202

Church of Scotland

Linked with Fowlis Wester (90)

3km (2 miles) from A9 on Dalreoch–Balgowan road

Gask Church was built in 1800, replacing an earlier church located a mile to the south. The architect of the stone-built and white-harled church was Richard Crichton. Interior reordered in 1950. Marble monument to the First World War and a stained-glass window marking the 53-year ministry of Rev. Dr James Martin. 2-manual Allen organ.

- Sunday: 11.30am in odd-numbered years, 10.00am in even-numbered years
- Open at all times

92 GLENDEVON PARISH CHURCH

Glendevon
FK14 7JY

NN 979 051

Church of Scotland

Linked with Dollar and Muckhart (both Clackmannanshire)

West side of A823, 1.6km (1 mile) north of Tormaukin Hotel

Simple whitewashed church of 1803. Large stained-glass window by Alf Webster of Glasgow, 1913, and small stained-glass window in memory of Rev. Alexander Taylor (1872–1949). Various memorial plaques. Pulpit and communion table and chair carved by Mr Philips of Tormaukin. Large gravestone to Jane Rutherford.

- Sunday: 11.15am
- Open daily

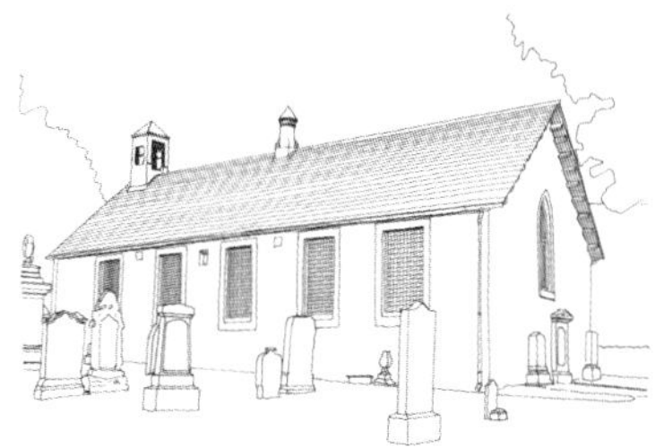

93 INCHTURE CHURCH

Carse Parish

Main Street
Inchture
PH14 9RN

NO 281 288
Church of Scotland
www.carsechurches.com

Linked with Abernyte (62), Kinnaird (99)

Off A90

The first mention of a church in Inchture is from the 12th century, when William the Lion granted the status of a parish church. The 1834–5 church was gutted by fire in 1890. The present Gothic T-plan church, designed by Duncan D. Stewart, factor of Rossie Estates, was erected the following year. Magnificent stained-glass window by Septimus Waugh was installed in 2000 to celebrate the Millennium.

- Sunday: 9.45am
- Open by arrangement (01828 686447)

INVERGOWRIE PARISH CHURCH

Main Street
Invergowrie
DD2 5BA

NO 346 304
Church of Scotland
www.invergowrie.f9.co.uk

Building opened 1909, architect John Robertson. Early Gothic with square tower and fine open timber roof. Pulpit and communion table of Austrian oak with carvings by local branch of YWCA. War-memorial bell, 1924. Stained-glass windows depicting Disruption minister Rev. R. S. Walker conducting open-air communion; and new window in chancel installed 2009 to celebrate centenary of building.

- Sunday: 11.00am; July and August also 9.30am
- Open Wednesday in July and August, afternoons or evenings (01382 561118)

ALL SOULS' CHURCH, INVERGOWRIE

59 Main Street
Invergowrie
DD2 5BA

NO 347 303

Scottish Episcopal

www.allsoulsinvergowrie.org/

On south side of Main Street

Red sandstone church with 42.5-metre (140-ft) spire, designed by Hippolyte Blanc, 1890, and built 1890–6. High altar has beautiful Italian marble reredos and crucifix. Lady Chapel contains altar from Rossie Priory Chapel. Sculptured Stations of the Cross. Embroidered wall hanging to celebrate centenary of consecration, 1996.

- Sunday: 10.00am; Wednesday: 10.15am
- Open during daylight hours (01382 562525)

   (in halls)

KETTINS PARISH CHURCH

Kettins
PH13 9JN

NO 238 390

Church of Scotland

www.ardler-kettins-meigle.org.uk

Linked with Meigle (103)

Off A923, 1.6km (1 mile) south-east of Coupar Angus

Founded in April 1249. The church stands on the site of one of six chapels established by a nearby Columban monastery. The present church dates from 1768, with the north wing added in 1870 and the tower in 1891. Belgian bell of 1519 now rests, complete with belfry, close to the west gable it once surmounted. Many interesting gravestones.

- Sunday: 11.30am
- Open by arrangement (01828 640074)

ST ADAMNAN'S CHURCH, KILMAVEONAIG

Ford Road
Blair Atholl
PH18 5SU

NN 874 658

Scottish Episcopal

www.htkepiscopalchurchesperthshire.org/

Blair Atholl, opposite Tilt Hotel

An Episcopal chapel rebuilt in 1794 by John Stewart on the site of the old parish church of Kilmaveonaig, 1591; has belonged to the Episcopal Communion without a break since the Revolution. Enlarged 1899 by the addition of the battlemented Gothic porch. Lorimer reredos added, 1912. Old bell, 1629, from Little Dunkeld Church.

- Sunday: 10.00am; 6.30pm, May to October
- Open by arrangement (01796 481230)

KINCLAVEN CHURCH

Kinclaven
PH1 4QW

NO 151 385

Church of Scotland

Linked with Caputh (75)

5km (3 miles) east of Murthly, 8km (5 miles) north-east of Stanley

Built 1848 on site of previous church. Mixed Romanesque and Tudor with a narthex at the west end and bellcote at the east end. Churchyard contains the war-memorial lychgate, 1919, by Reginald Fairlie, and some table tombs of the 17th century and later. Built into the churchyard wall is the monument to Alexander Cabel (Campbell), Bishop of Brechin, 1608.

- Sunday: 9.45am
- Open by arrangement (01738 710548)

99 KINNAIRD CHURCH

Carse Parish

Kinnaird
PH14 9QY

NO 243 287

Church of Scotland

www.carsechurches.com

Linked with Abernyte (62), Inchture (93)

Off A90

Commanding view across the Carse of Gowrie. The current church dates from 1815, but evidence exists of an earlier church on this site going back to at least 1153. The Thriepland family were early patrons, and their memorials dating from 1669 remain in the churchyard today.

- Sunday: 9.30am
- Open by arrangement (01828 686447)

100 KINROSS PARISH CHURCH

10 Station Road
Kinross
KY13 8TG

NO 117 023

Church of Scotland

www.kinrossparishchurch.org/

Station Road links the M90 with Kinross

Tudor Gothic-style church with a tall west tower by George Angus, 1831–2, using the almost identical designs of Kingskettle and Kincardine. The apparently cruciform plan cleverly disguises a square, Georgian, preaching interior, flooded with light. Modernised 2005 but retaining the overall interior form. Memorial tablets to the Grahams of Kinross, and a stained-glass window (James Ballantine II, 1926).

- Sunday: 10.30am
- Open usually 10.00am–12.00 noon Monday to Friday; but contact church in advance (01577 862570)

LITTLE DUNKELD CHURCH

School Lane
Little Dunkeld
PH8 0RQ

NO 028 423

Church of Scotland

www.dunkeldcathedral.org.uk/little_dunkeld.htm

Linked with St Anne's, Dowally (83), Dunkeld Cathedral (86)

Close to Tay Bridge

Designed and built by John Stewart in 1798, it is a typical 18th-century preaching kirk. The graveyard contains interesting stones, including two 'Adam and Eve' stones and Neil Gow's grave. The interior has been altered and refurbished and has a bright and colourful look.

- Sunday: 11.00am mid-November to Palm Sunday; also 6.30pm on 1st Sunday in March and December
- Open by arrangement (01350 727614)

LONGFORGAN PARISH CHURCH

Main Street
Longforgan
DD2 5ET

NO 309 300

Church of Scotland

www.carsechurches.org.uk

There has been a church on this site for at least 900 years. The tower is dated 1690 and has an 8-sided steeple and unusual clock. The main building, by John Paterson, dates from 1795; the chancel, by Alexander Hutcheson, from 1900. Windows from 1900–2003, wood carving by Sir Robert Lorimer, a unique pipe organ and the remains of a medieval font. Several interesting tombstones from the 12th century are preserved in the church.

- Sunday: 11.00am
- Open by arrangement (01382 360294)

103 MEIGLE PARISH CHURCH

The Square
Meigle
PH12 8RT

NO 287 446

Church of Scotland

www.ardler-kettins-meigle.org.uk

Linked with Kettins (96)

Rebuilt in 1870 by John Carver after fire destroyed the pre-Reformation stone church of 1431. Stands on the ancient site of a turf church erected by Columban missionaries around AD 606. Fine stone font. Interesting graveyard. Pictish stones in adjacent museum (Historic Scotland).

- Sunday: 10.00am
- Open by arrangement (01828 640074)

104 ORWELL PARISH CHURCH, MILNATHORT

North Street
Milnathort
KY13 7YF

NO 121 051

Church of Scotland

www.culdees.org.uk/orwell portmoakchurch/

Linked with Portmoak (120)

Church constructed 1729 using stone from the Old Kirk of Orwell on the banks of Loch Leven. The roof was raised and the present windows, floor and seating installed and galleries added in 1769. The interior is enhanced by embroidered banners and kneelers crafted by members of the Church. Interesting gravestones in the graveyard.

- Sunday: 11.30am
- Open by arrangement

105 MORENISH CHAPEL

Morenish
FK21 8TY

NN 608 356

Church of Scotland

Linked with Killin and Balquhidder (both Stirlingshire)

On A827, 5km (3 miles) north-east of Killin

Built in 1902 by Aline White Todd in memory of her daughter Elvira, who died in childbirth. The central piece of the chapel is the magnificent east window by Tiffany in heavily leaded tracery, and sumptuous stained glass showing Moses receiving the ten commandments on Mount Sinai.

- Sunday: 3.00pm on 1st Sunday of the month during summer
- Open by arrangement (01567 820247)

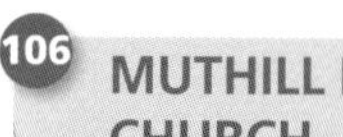

106 MUTHILL PARISH CHURCH

Station Road
Muthill
PH5 2AS

NN 868 171

Church of Scotland

5km (3 miles) south of Crieff on A822

Replaced the 12th-century church (still existing). Built in 1826 in Gothic style to a design by Gillespie Graham, nicknamed 'Pinnacle' Graham by those less enthusiastic for the sprockets of 19th-century Gothic. The pulpit canopy is similarly sprocketed.

- Sunday: 11.30am
- Open by arrangement (01764 681362)

107 ST JAMES'S CHURCH, MUTHILL

Station Road
Muthill
PH5 2AR

NN 869 170

Scottish Episcopal

www.stkessogs.co.uk

Linked with St Kessog's, Auchterarder (68)

Opposite primary school

Tall, cruciform Gothic church of 1836, designed by R. & R. Dickson of Edinburgh. Oldest Episcopal church in the area. Numerous family crests of historic interest and memorial tablets. Brass lectern, altar rails and stained glass, all probably by R. T. N. Speir. Organ by Wadsworth & Bros, 1888.

- Sunday: 11.00am January to June, 9.30am July to December
- Open by arrangement (01764 662525)

108 ST JOHN'S KIRK OF PERTH

St John Place
Perth
PH1 5SH

NO 119 235

Church of Scotland

www.st-johns-kirk.co.uk

Linked with St Leonard's-in-the-Fields, Perth (113)

Burgh church of Perth dedicated to John the Baptist and consecrated in 1242 on site of earlier church. Divided into three churches after the Reformation and restored 1923–6 by Sir Robert Lorimer. Good examples of modern stained glass, including window of Knox Chapel by Douglas Strachan. Statue of John the Baptist by Indian sculptor Fanindra Bose, and tapestry by Archie Brennan of Dovecot Studios, Edinburgh. Nave with barrel vaulting has carvings of events in the life of Christ. Glass screen at west door installed, 1988. Organ by Rothwell, 1926, rebuilt 1986 by Edmonstone.

- Sunday: 9.30am
- Open weekdays May to September; other times by arrangement (01738 638482)

109 ST NINIAN'S CATHEDRAL, PERTH

**North Methven Street
Perth
PH1 5PP**

NO 116 237

Scottish Episcopal

www.perthcathedral.co.uk

First cathedral to be built after the Reformation, being consecrated in 1850; architect William Butterfield. Choir, crossing, transepts and part of the nave are to his design; west front, apse, chapter-house and cloister are by L. J. & F. L. Pearson, 1911. Richly decorated interior. Baldacchino in Cornish granite, fine wooden statue of the Risen Christ and interesting stained glass. Founder's window, the font, rood screen and one of the banners by Sir Ninian Comper.

- Sunday: 8.00am and 11.00am; Monday to Friday: 9.00am; Wednesday: 11.00am
- Open Monday to Friday 9.00am–5.00pm (01738 632053)

110 ST JOHN THE BAPTIST, PERTH

**20 Melville Street
Perth
PH1 5PY**

NO 114 241

Roman Catholic

Linked with St Mary Magdalene, Perth (115)

Near main police station

Traditional building of 1832, enlarged 1896 by Andrew Heiton. Presbytery 1932 by Reginald Fairlie. Church renovated 1967 for new liturgy by Peter Whiston of Edinburgh, and many previous accretions removed.

- Saturday: 6.30pm; Sunday: 9.00am, 11.00am and 6.30pm
- Open 8.00am–dusk (01738 622241)

C   

111 KINNOULL PARISH CHURCH, PERTH

Dundee Road
Perth
PH2 7EY

NO 123 236

Church of Scotland

www.kinnoullparishchurch.co.uk

Across the Tay from town centre

Designed 1827 by Edinburgh architect William Burn in a neo-perpendicular style. The glory of the interior is the stained glass, especially the west window based on a series of paintings of the Parables of Our Lord by Sir John Everett Millais. Three other windows by Douglas Strachan.

- Sunday: 10.30am
- Open by arrangement (01738 634785)

NORTH CHURCH, PERTH

209 High Street
Perth
PH1 5PB

NO 116 237

Church of Scotland

www.northchurch.org.uk

Junction with Mill Street

The church was founded in 1747 following the 'Burgher' and 'Antiburgher' controversy that split the Secession churches in the 18th century. Following unions with other churches, the North Church became Church of Scotland in 1929. A pleasant city-centre church completed in 1880 by T. L. Watson of Glasgow in Italian Romanesque style.

- Sunday: 9.30am, 11.00am and 6.30pm; Thursday: 1.00pm
- Open by arrangement (01738 443216)

ST LEONARD'S-IN-THE-FIELDS, PERTH

**Marshall Place
Perth
PH2 8AG**

NO 117 232

Church of Scotland

www.stleonardsinthefields.org

Linked with St John's Kirk of Perth (108)

Fine example of the late Gothic Revival by John J. Stevenson of London, opened in 1885 as St Leonard's Free Church. An impressive Scots Gothic church with outstanding architectural features of the crown tower and the heavy buttresses. The organ, Bryceson 1881, which came from North Morningside Church in Edinburgh, was installed in the centenary year, 1985.

- Sunday: 11.15am
- Open by arrangement (01738 633452)

ST JOHN'S EPISCOPAL, PERTH

**Princes Street
Perth
PH2 8LJ**

NO 119 233

Scottish Episcopal

www.episcopal-perth.org.uk

The present site has been used for worship since 1800. Present building designed by John Hay of Liverpool, 1850–1, in English Decorated Gothic style. Cruciform church with a tower between the nave and north transept. Many stained-glass windows, sculptures by Miss Mary Grant, chancel arch carved by Heiton. Fine Harrison & Harrison organ, 1971.

- Sunday: 8.00am and 10.30am; Thursday: 11.00am
- Open by arrangement (01738 634999)

115 ST MARY MAGDALENE, PERTH

Glenearn Road
Perth
PH2 0BD

NO 113 226

Roman Catholic

Linked with St John the Baptist RC, Perth (110)

Modern building (1958–9), attractive in its simplicity, designed by Peter Whiston of Edinburgh. Very interesting window by William Wilson and crucifix by Benno Schotz.

- Sunday: 10.00am
- Open by arrangement (01738 622241)

116 ST MATTHEW'S, PERTH

West Church

Tay Street
Perth
PH1 5LQ

NO 121 235

Church of Scotland

www.stmatthewsperth.co.uk

Early English Gothic by John Honeyman, 1871; originally West Free Church. Its impressive steeple is a much-photographed landmark of Perth. Organ by J. W. Walker. In 1965, after the union of four churches, stained-glass windows, plaques and memorial tablets from the four churches were incorporated in the existing West Church, now St Matthew's.

- Sunday: 11.00am
- Open daily 9.00am–12.00 noon (01738 630725)

117 PITLOCHRY CHURCH

**Church Road
Pitlochry
PH16 5EB**

NN 940 582

Church of Scotland

www.pitlochrychurchofscotland.org.uk

The 'church with the clock', 100 metres from main street. Cruciform church with tower designed in 1884 by C. & L. Ower of Dundee. The porch was added in 1995, built of stone from Pitlochry East Church. Seating arranged in a part-circle around the communion table. Monument to Alexander Duff, 19th-century missionary.

- Sunday: 10.30am
- Open mid-June to mid-September, Monday to Friday 10.00am–12.00 noon (01796 472160)

 HOLY TRINITY EPISCOPAL, PITLOCHRY

**Perth Road
Pitlochry
PH16 5LY**

NN 946 578

Scottish Episcopal

www.htkepiscopalchurches perthshire.org

Opened 1858, architect C. Buckeridge of Oxford; nave extended 1890. Organ by Hele (1903). Reredos by Sir Ninian Comper, 1893, richly coloured in red and gold. Stained-glass windows by various artists including E. Kempe, Clayton & Bell, A. Ballantine & Son, John Hardman & Co. and Alexander L. Russell. Lychgate built c. 1925.

- Sunday: 11.30am
- Open mid-June to mid-September, Thursday and Friday, 10.00am–12.00 noon and 2.00–4.00pm (01796 472745)

119 PITLOCHRY BAPTIST CHURCH

Atholl Road
Pitlochry
PH16 5BX

NN 942 580

Baptist

www.pitlochrybaptistchurch.org

Next to Tourist Information Centre

Founded in 1878 and originally meeting in a joiner's shop, the Pitlochry Fellowship built this church in 1884 to a design by Crombie of Edinburgh. Cruciform church with extensive halls. Today's congregation welcomes visitors from across the world all year round.

- Sunday: 11.00am and 6.30pm
- Open by arrangement (01796 472127)

120 PORTMOAK PARISH CHURCH

Scotlandwell
KY13 9HY

NO 183 019

Church of Scotland

www.culdees.org.uk/orwell portmoakchurch/

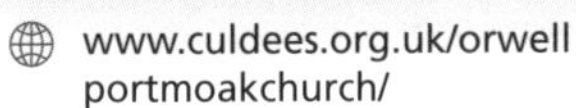

Linked with Orwell Church, Milnathort (104)

1.6km (1 mile) west of Scotlandwell

The present building, dated 1832, is the third on the site. Rectangular in plan, with a horseshoe gallery with the pulpit on the long south wall flanked by tall windows. The bell is dated 1642, and the Celtic crosses are of the 10th or 11th centuries. Memorial stone in the graveyard to Michael Bruce (1746–67), author of several of the Scripture paraphrases used in Church of Scotland worship.

- Sunday: 10.00am
- Open by arrangement

SCONE OLD PARISH CHURCH

Burnside
Scone
PH2 6LP

NO 134 256

Church of Scotland

www.sconeold.org.uk

Next to the school

Church built in 1286 near to Scone Palace. Moved to present site in 1806 using stone from original building. Stormont Pew of 1616. Memorial to David Douglas, botanist, in graveyard.

- Sunday: 11.00am
- Open by arrangement (01738 551549)

OLD CHURCH OF RANNOCH

Kinloch Rannoch
PH16 5QA

NN 663 585

Church of Scotland

Linked with Braes of Rannoch (74), Foss (89)

South Loch Road

A Thomas Telford church of 1829, extensively altered and enlarged in 1893 when the rose window was inserted and porch and vestry were added. Wooden-beamed roof, stained-glass window; hourglass by pulpit.

- Sunday: 11.30am
- Open daily 10.00am–dusk or by arrangement (01882 632381)

  (by arrangement)  

ST MADOES AND KINFAUNS CHURCH

St Madoes
PH2 7NF

NO 197 213

Church of Scotland

Off A90, 5km (3 miles) east of Perth

Built 1799 on the site of earlier churches and refurbished in 1923. T-plan church with laird's gallery. New vestry and entrance hall by David Murdoch of Methven, 1996. Interesting historic graveyard with 18th-century gravestones of sculptural merit. Pictish St Madoes Stone now on display in Perth Museum and Art Gallery. Contemporary embroidered pulpit falls.

- Sunday: 11.00am September to May, 10.00am June to August
- Open 1st Sunday of the month, June to September 1.00–4.00pm (01738 621305)

STANLEY PARISH CHURCH

King Street
Stanley
PH1 4ND

NO 110 329

Church of Scotland

Built in 1828 by local mill-owners the Buchanan family for mill-workers, the Georgian Gothic church seated 1,000. It was adapted in 1962 and incorporated a new pew arrangement. The halls which are below the sanctuary were refurbished in 1997. The vestibule houses the war memorial.

- Sunday: 11.30am except last Sunday of the month
- Open by arrangement (01738 828247)

125 ST ANDREW'S CHURCH, STRATHTAY

Strathtay
PH9 0PJ

NN 910 534

Scottish Episcopal

Linked with St Mary's, Birnam (71)

On A827 between Ballinluig and Aberfeldy

Simple Gothic church of chancel and nave with octagonal tower, replacing a cast-iron church. The chancel was built in 1888 and the nave added in 1919. A vestibule and hall were added in 1982. Heavily carved woodwork on pulpit, lectern and priest's prayer desk. Lovely stained glass by Thomas Willement. A free-standing belfry was provided in 1995.

- Sunday: 11.30am
- Open by arrangement (01887 840212)

126 TENANDRY CHURCH

Tenandry
PH16 5LH

NN 911 615

Church of Scotland

www.geocities/athollkirks

800 metres (½ mile) north of Garry Bridge (B8019)

Small country church of traditional design, built in 1836 of stone and slate. Traditional galleried interior with pews of 1896. Fine view of the Pass of Killiecrankie from the road above the church.

- Sunday: 10.00am
- Open daily (01796 473252)

127 TIBBERMORE CHURCH

Tibbermore
PH1 1QJ

NO 052 234

Former Church of Scotland

www.srct.org.uk

400 metres (¼ mile) south of Tibbermore crossroads

The present church dates from 1632, though the site has been a place of worship from the Middle Ages onwards. The church was remodelled and enlarged in 1789 to designs by James Scobie, made T-plan in 1808, and the interior refurnished in 1874. The present interior is little altered since that date. Many monuments of interest, in particular the exceptional memorial to James Ritchie, displaying his curling equipment and the recumbent figure of his bull. Transferred to the ownership of the Scottish Redundant Churches Trust in 2001.

- Occasional services
- Open by arrangement (01334 472032)

128 WEEM CHURCH

Weem
PH15 2LD

NN 844 498

Church of Scotland

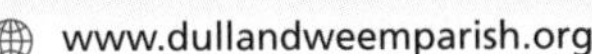

www.dullandweemparish.org

Linked with Aberfeldy (61), Amulree (66)

1.6km (1 mile) north of Aberfeldy on B846

The style of this beautiful stone building indicates its origin as an Episcopal church of the late 19th century; the ancient former church of Dull and Weem was 5km (3 miles) west. Interesting organ. A small hall was added to the north in 1990, during the construction of which the ancient well of Weem was discovered.

- Sunday: 10.00am
- Open by arrangement (01887 820656)

Index

References are to each church's entry number in the gazetteer.